September 1557

New and Selected Poems
1966–1988

ECCO'S MODERN EUROPEAN POETRY SERIES

Selected Poems 1966–1988 by Douglas Dunn

Report from the Besieged City by Zbigniew Herbert

Selected Poems by Zbigniew Herbert

Bells in Winter by Czeslaw Milosz

The Collected Poems 1931–1987 by Czeslaw Milosz

The Separate Notebooks by Czeslaw Milosz

Unattainable Earth by Czeslaw Milosz

Selected Poems 1968–1986 by Paul Muldoon

Hard Labor by Cesare Pavese

Poems of Fernando Pessoa

Exile and Return: Selected Poems 1967–1974 by Yannis Ritsos

The Selected Poems of Tomaž Šalamun

Selected Poems by Tomas Tranströmer

Forthcoming

The Selected Poems of Robert Desnos
translated by William Kulik and Carolyn Forché

K. S. in Lakeland: New and Selected Poems
by Michael Hofmann

The Selected Poems of Marina Tsvetaeva
translated by Joseph Brodsky and Mark Strand

With the Skin: The Poems of Aleksander Wat
translated and edited by Czeslaw Milosz and Leonard Nathaı

Douglas Dunn

New and Selected Poems
1966–1988

THE ECCO PRESS
New York

Library of Congress Cataloging in Publication Data

Dunn, Douglas.
Selected poems, 1966–1988.
(Modern European poetry series)
I. Title. II. Series.
PR6054.U54A6 1989   821'.914   88–33467

ISBN 0-88001-177-7 (cloth)
ISBN 0-88001-178-5 (paper)

Contents

from ELEGIES

from NORTHLIGHT

from
Terry Street

The Clothes Pit

The young women are obsessed with beauty.
Their old-fashioned sewing machines rattle in Terry
  Street.
They must keep up, they must keep up.

They wear teasing skirts and latest shoes,
Lush, impermanent coats, American cosmetics.
But they lack intellectual grooming.

In the culture of clothes and little philosophies,
They only have clothes. They do not need to be seen
Carrying a copy of *International Times,*

Or the Liverpool Poets, the wish to justify their looks
With things beyond themselves. They mix up colours,
And somehow they are often fat and unlovely.

They don't get high on pot, but get sick on cheap
Spanish Burgundy, or beer in rampant pubs,
And come home supported and kissed and bad-tempered.

But they have clothes, bright enough to show they dream
Of places other than this, an inarticulate paradise,
Eating exotic fowl in sunshine with courteous boys.

Three girls go down the street with the summer wind.
The litter of pop rhetoric blows down Terry Street,
Bounces past their feet, into their lives.

New Light on Terry Street

First sunshine for three weeks, and children come out
From their tents of chairs and old sheets,

Living room traffic jams, and battlefields of redcoat soldiers,
To expand, run on unsteady legs in and out of shades.

Up terraces of slums, young gum-chewing mothers sit
Outside on their thrones of light. Their radios,

Inside or placed on window ledges, grow hot
With sun and electricity. Shielding their eyes from sun

They talk above music, knitting or pushing prams
Over gentle, stone inches. Under clawed chairs

Cats sleep in the furry shade. Children bounce balls
Up into their dreams of sand, and the sea they have not seen.

Becoming tired, the fascination of wheels takes them.
They pedal their trikes slowly through dust in hollows,

Quietly give up cheek to old men, sing with sly voices.
A half-heard love song idles on the wind.

Yet there is no unrest. The dust is so fine.
You hardly notice you have grown too old to cry out for
                                                        change.

The Patricians

In small backyards old men's long underwear
Drips from sagging clotheslines.
The other stuff they take in bundles to the Bendix.

There chatty women slot their coins and joke
About the grey unmentionables absent.
The old men weaken in the steam and scratch at their
    rough chins.

Suppressing coughs and stiffnesses, they pedal bikes
On low gear slowly, in their faces
The effort to be upright, a dignity

That fits inside the smell of aromatic pipes.
Walking their dogs, the padded beats of pocket watches,
Muffled under ancient overcoats, silence their hearts.

They live watching each other die, passing each other
In their white scarves, too long known to talk,
Waiting for the inheritance of the oldest, a right to power.

The street's patricians, they are ignored.
Their anger proves something, their disenchantments
Settle round me like a cold fog.

They are the individualists of our time.
They know no fashions, copy nothing but their minds.
Long ago, they gave up looking in mirrors.

Dying in their sleep, they lie undiscovered.
The howling of their dogs brings the sniffing police,
Their middle-aged children from the new estates.

Men of Terry Street

They come in at night, leave in the early morning.
I hear their footsteps, the ticking of bicycle chains,
Sudden blasts of motorcycles, whimpering of vans.
Somehow I am either in bed, or the curtains are drawn.

This masculine invisibility makes gods of them,
A pantheon of boots and overalls.
But when you see them, home early from work
Or at their Sunday leisure, they are too tired

And bored to look long at comfortably.
It hurts to see their faces, too sad or too jovial.
They quicken their step at the smell of cooking,
They hold up their children and sing to them.

Incident in the Shop

Not tall, her good looks unstylized,
She wears no stockings, or uses cosmetic.

I sense beneath her blouse
The slow expanse of unheld breasts.

I feel the draughts on her legs,
The nip of cheap detergent on her hands.

Under her bed, forgotten winter bulbs
Die of thirst, in the grip of a wild dust.

Her husband beats her. Old women
Talk of it behind her back, watching her.

She buys the darkest rose I ever saw
And tucks its stem into her plastic belt.

A Removal from Terry Street

On a squeaking cart, they push the usual stuff,
A mattress, bed ends, cups, carpets, chairs,
Four paperback westerns. Two whistling youths
In surplus US Army battle-jackets
Remove their sister's goods. Her husband
Follows, carrying on his shoulders the son
Whose mischief we are glad to see removed,
And pushing, of all things, a lawnmower.
There is no grass in Terry Street. The worms
Come up cracks in concrete yards in moonlight.
That man, I wish him well. I wish him grass.

On Roofs of Terry Street

Television aerials, Chinese characters
In the lower sky, wave gently in the smoke.

Nest-building sparrows peck at moss,
Urban flora and fauna, soft, unscrupulous.

Rain drying on the slates shines sometimes.
A builder is repairing someone's leaking roof.

He kneels upright to rest his back.
His trowel catches the light and becomes precious.

From the Night-Window

The night rattles with nightmares.
Children cry in the close-packed houses,
A man rots in his snoring.
On quiet feet, policemen test doors.
Footsteps become people under streetlamps.
Drunks return from parties,
Sounding of empty bottles and old songs.
Young women come home
And disappear into white beds
At the edge of the night.
All windows open, this hot night,
And the sleepless, smoking in the dark,
Making small red lights at their mouths,
Count the years of their marriages.

Sunday Morning Among the Houses of Terry Street

On the quiet street, Saturday night's fag-packets,
Balls of fish and chip newspaper, bottles
Placed neatly on window sills, beside cats.

A street of oilstains and parked motorbikes,
Wet confectionery wrappers becoming paste,
Things doing nothing, ending, rejected.

Revellers return tieless, or with hairdos deceased,
From parties, paying taxis in the cold,
Unsmiling in the fogs of deflated mirth.

Neighbours in pyjamas watch them from upstairs,
Chewing on pre-breakfast snacks,
Waiting for kettles to boil, wives quit the lav.

Men leave their beds to wash and eat,
Fumble with Sunday papers and radio knobs,
Leaving in their beds their wives and fantasies,

In bedside cups their teeth, their smiles.
Drinkers sleep into a blank sobriety,
Still talking to the faces in the smoke,

Women they regretted they were too drunk to touch,
Sucking tastes in their mouths, their mossy teeth.
Into the street come early-risen voices,

The Salvation Army's brass dulled in sunlessness
And breath of singers the colour of tubas.
Dog obbligatos rise from warm corners.

Behind the houses, antique plumbing
Coughs and swallows Sunday morning's flush
Down to Hull's underworld, its muddy roots.

A city of disuse, a sink, a place,
Without people it would be like the sea-bottom.
Beneath the street, a thundering of mud.

After Closing Time

Here they come, the agents of rot,
The street tarts and their celebrating trawlermen,
Singing or smoking, carrying bottles,
In a staggered group ten minutes before snow.

Winter

Recalcitrant motorbikes;
Dog-shit under frost; a coughing woman;
The old men who cannot walk briskly groaning
On the way back from their watchmen's huts.

Young Women in Rollers

Because it's wet, the afternoon is quiet.
Children, pacified with sweets inside
Their small houses, stroke travelling cats
From the kingdom of dustbins and warm smells.

Young women come to visit their married friend.
Waiting for their hair to set beneath thin scarves,
They walk about in last year's fashions,
Stockingless, in coats and old shoes.

They look strong, white-legged creatures
With nothing to do but talk of what it is to love
And sing words softly to the new tunes,
The type who burst each other's blackheads

In the street and look in handbag mirrors
While they walk, not talking of the weather,
Who call across the street they're not wearing knickers,
But blush when they pass you alone.

This time they see me at my window, among books,
A specimen under glass, being protected,
And laugh at me watching them.
They minuet to Mozart playing loudly

On the afternoon Third. They mock me thus,
They mime my culture. A landlord stares.
All he has worked for is being destroyed.
The slum rent-masters are at one with Pop.

The movements they imagine go with minuet
Stay patterned on the air. I can see soot,
It floats. The whiteness of their legs has changed
Into something that floats, become like cloth.

They disappear into the house they came to visit.
Out of the open door rush last year's hits,
The music they listen to, that takes up their time
In houses that are monuments to entertainment.

I want to be touched by them, know their lives,
Dance in my own style, learn something new.
At night, I even dream of ideal communities.
Why do they live where they live, the rich and the poor?

Tonight, when their hair is ready, after tea,
They'll slip through laws and the legs of policemen.
I won't be there, I'll be reading books elsewhere.
There are many worlds, there are many laws.

The Silences

It is urban silence, it is not true silence.
The main road, growling in the distance,
Continuous, is absorbed into it;
The birds, their noises become lost in it;
Faint, civilized music decorates it.

These are edges round a quiet centre where lives are lived,
Children brought up, where television aerial fixers come,
Or priests on black bikes to lecture the tardy.
If you turn your back on it, people are only noises,
Coughs, footsteps, conversations, hands working.

They are a part of the silence of places,
The people who live here, working, falling asleep,
In a place removed one style in time outwith
The trend of places. They are like a lost tribe.
Dogs bark when strangers come, with rent books, or
    free gifts.

They move only a little from where they are fixed.
Looking at worn clothes, they sense impermanence.
They have nothing to do with where they live, the silence
    tells them.
They have looked at it so long, with such disregard,
It is baked now over their eyes like a crust.

A Window Affair

We were looking at the same things,
Men on bikes, the litter round the drain,
The sparrows eating in the frozen shade.

We heard the same inweave of random noise,
The chant of children's games, and waiting cars
Of salesmen and collectors ticking over.

This was weekday flirtation, through the glass,
The love of eyes and silence, in which you cannot touch
Or talk, a useless love for the bored and tired.

Her window caught the winter sun and shone.
I imagined everything, the undressing, love,
The coy sleep. But there was nothing to say.

There were two faces, and they passed each other
Like shillings in circulation. Untouchable,
She was far away, in a world of foul language,

Two children, the television set in the corner,
As common as floral wallpaper or tea,
Her husband in at six to feed the greyhounds.

I used to crave the ideal life of Saturdays and Sundays,
A life of everything in a gay, short-lived country
Of high-living among the northern bricks,

Where people come out rested into the rain,
Wearing smiles as if they were expensive clothes,
Their bodies clean and warm and their jobs indoors.

But some ideals have passed far out of my reach,
The goodwill became full of holes like a sieve.
I grasp only the hard things, windows, contempt.

I could not kiss that face, the glowing mask
Of those who have been too much entertained,
That laughs the sour laugh and smells of food.

It's come to this, that in this time, this place,
There is a house I feel I have to leave,
Because my life is cracked, and in a room

Stares out of windows at a window face,
Thin shifts of dust on the sunning glass,
And does not want to love, and does not care.

Envoi

Why did I bring you to this Hull,
This rancid and unbeautiful
Surprise of damp and Englishness?
Mad for an education, for poetry,
I studied at our window,
My mind dying in shy cadences.
What cost of life was there, in poverty,
In my outlaw depressions, in your coping
With lonely, studious bohemia!

Now I choose to remember
Bus-rides together into Holderness,
Exploring the hedgerowed heat
On country walks by fields of mustard.
That view was broad and circular
Where everywhere seemed everywhere!

A curse on me I did not write with joy.

(1981)

from
The Happier Life

The River Through the City

The river of coloured lights, black stuff
The tired city rests its jewels on.
Bad carnival, men and women
Drown themselves under the bridges.
Death-splash, and after, the river wears
The neon flowers of suicides.
Prints of silence ripple where they went in.
An old man rows a black boat and slides past
Unnoticed, a god in an oilskin coat.
He feeds the uncatchable black fish.
They know where Hitler is hiding.
They know the secrets behind sordid events
In Central Europe, in America and Asia,
And who is doing what for money.
They keep files on petty thieves, spies,
Adulterers and their favourite bureaucrats.
That's one old man who's nobody's uncle.
That's one fish you don't want with your chips.
Iron doors bang shut in the sewers.

The Friendship of Young Poets

There must have been more than just one of us,
But we never met. Each kept in his world of loss
The promise of literary days, the friendship
Of poets, mysterious, that sharing of books
And talking in whispers in crowded bars
Suspicious enough to be taken for love.

We never met. My youth was as private
As the bank at midnight, and in its safety
No talking behind backs, no one alike enough
To be pretentious with and quote lines at.

There is a boat on the river now, and
Two young men, one rowing, one reading aloud.
Their shirt sleeves fill with wind, and from the oars
Drop scales of perfect river like melting glass.

Nights of Sirius

Unknown men tonight will put
One last hand to a life's work,
Hobbyhorse or a pedantic search
For private seriousness;
Or add a wise last paragraph
To the privately published
Volume of family history,
Put back on the cherished shelf
Of an eccentric library
To be read in ten years' time
By a bookish grandson.

High summer, and dog-star nights
Are still and hot, accepting death
And notebooks, snapshot albums,
Treasured books and objects,
A chair, his favourite tie –
Possessions the dead have left,
What pleased them, passed their time,
And shall, like wives, preserve
Their marks of ownership,
Ways of what it felt like to be theirs,
Touch, pulse, the smell of hands.

The Musical Orchard

Girls on mopeds rode to Fécamp parties,
And as they passed the ripened orchard
Cheered an old man's music,
Not knowing it was sad.
Those French tunes on the saxophone,
The music inside fruit!

Backwaters

They are silent places, dilapidated cities
Obscure to the nation, their names spoken of
In the capital with distinct pejorative overtones.

For some, places mean coming to or going from,
Comedians and singers with their suitcases
Packed with signed photographs of themselves;

Businessmen in sharp suits, come to buy and sell,
Still seeking their paradise of transactions,
The bottomless market, where the mugs live.

For others, places are sites for existence,
Where roads slow down and come to a stop
Outside where it's good to be, particular places

Where instantly recognized people live,
The buses are a familiar colour and life is
Utterly civilian, all uniforms

Merely the kind insignia of postmen
And meter readers. There complacency means
Men are almost the same, and almost right.

And for a few, places are only the dumps
They end up in, backwaters, silent places,
The cheapest rooms of the cheapest towns.

These darker streets, like the bad days in our lives,
Are where the stutterers hide, the ugly and clubfooted,
The radically nervous who are hurt by crowds.

They love the sunlight at street corners
And the tough young men walking out of it,
And the police patrol. Poverty makes fools of them.

They have done so little they are hardly aware of themselves.
Unmissed, pensioned, at the far end of all achievements,
In their kiln-baked rooms, they are permanent.

Supreme Death

Fishing on a wide river from a boat
A corpse was caught, her black hair like a huge weed,
The hook stuck in a black shroud strangely marked.

There were others. Hundreds gathered round the boat,
Some turning, their white faces like pillows.
I lost my oars, and the river quickened.

On the towpath, men in their hundreds
Ran with the tide, singing, and pushing,
When they felt like it, some poor fool into the river.

Death, the best of all mysteries, layer
After layer is peeled off your secrecy
Until all that is left is an inexplicable ooze.

Too late, it is myself.
Too late, my heart is a beautiful top.
Too late, all the dead in the river are my friends.

The Hunched

They will not leave me, the lives of other people.
I wear them near my eyes like spectacles.
Sullen magnates, hunched into chins and overcoats
In the back seats of their large cars;
Scholars, so conscientious, as if to escape
Things too real, names too easily read,
Preferring language stuffed with difficulties;
And children, furtive with their own parts;
A lonely glutton in the sunlit corner
Of an empty Chinese restaurant;
A coughing woman, leaning on a wall,
Her wedding-ring finger in her son's cold hand,
In her back the invisible arch of death.
What makes them laugh, who lives with them?

I stooped to lace a shoe, and they all came back,
Mysterious people without names or faces,
Whose lives I guess about, whose dangers tease.
And not one of them has anything at all to do with me.

Emblems

Rich nights in another climate –
White tables and the best Moselle,
A garden that slopes to a clear river;
Style I cannot make and was not born to claim.

And the factory is humming at full production
Just over the hill, making money,
Whispering, a big fish without eyes,
The most profound unhappiness.

Modern Love

It is summer, and we are in a house
That is not ours, sitting at a table
Enjoying minutes of a rented silence,
The upstairs people gone. The pigeons lull
To sleep the under-tens and invalids,
The tree shakes out its shadows to the grass,
The roses rove through the wilds of my neglect.
Our lives flap, and we have no hope of better
Happiness than this, not much to show for love
Than how we are, or how this evening is,
Unpeopled, silent, and where we are alive
In a domestic love, seemingly alone,
All other lives worn down to trees and sunlight,
Looking forward to a visit from the cat.

from
Love or Nothing

Winter Graveyard

Mossed obelisks and moss-gloved curves,
Uncherishable headstones
Rise from the dead place at a time of death.
A swarm of fissured angels sweeps over
Unremarkable civilians,
Magnates of no inheritance;
In depths of briar and ivy
Their utterly negative remains –
Dried convolvulus,
A bush of nerves sprouted
From lost anatomies.

Survivors of scattered families
Can't get at inscriptions.
When did Frederick die? Or Emily?
They need to know. Relatives
Underfoot impart a sad feeling
Worth expeditions
Sometimes beaten back by the strength
Of wild entanglements
Pensioners declare is neglect, unprincipled
Spite of generation for generation,
And imply their own regret.

How can they bear to know they are
Now similarly fated
In a city not even a metropolis,
And their cross a broken ornament?
Even that era of grand proprieties,
Domain of the picture-hook and claw-footed table,
Its offering servants,
Is sunk and forgotten,
Submerged under midget Gothic.
Fast sycamores grow
Upright out of Victorian creeper.

This is a door to Victoria's heaven.
Sinking one's face in a cushion,
Sharing, as if from an alms box,
Love preserved in Death,
And its hundred-thousand sentiments –
The man who came from the house
With the dancers to talk of the summer,
A soldier who told Edwardian merchants
Of a minor campaign in Assam.
They dance now to secret ragtime
In red-plush joints.

Once they were blue citizenry
At the ends of streets, in horse-traffic.
If I shut my eyes
They are still there, in the same stillness,
The same harmonious dusk
Of a generation whose male children –
Young in 1914 –
Are not buried here
But died abroad defending an Empire's
Affectionate stability
And an industry of lies.

Rank everlastingness
Mud-buttered –
Money is this,
One old penny at the edge of a grave,
Shrill starlings over
Columns and sarcophagi, as many as
The corners hiding God
Here, in his formal dump.
Rubbish of names under vomit of moss;
Inscriptions incised
In thin velvet

Rinse their loving vocabularies
In the light of dreams.
And I am momentarily disabled by
The thought that this is real – pink sky
Behind the black upreaching trees,
Aspirations of beauty and love
Disregarding corroded vulgarity
And farcical monuments
To sanctities not worth the enshrinement
That outlast memory and money.
And a white bird leaves a bare tree.

Winter Orchard

Five days of fog over snow,
Thinning, thickening, thinning
Before dark,
Its last substantial grit,
A breath with industry on it.

Blank miseries
Of the average dead;
Miscellaneous, unspectacular visitation;
Spiritual dregs
Out of the gutters of what-drab-Heaven,

The City of what-suburbanly-managerial-God?
Cold torpor of questions,
Revenge of the unfructified,
Yesterday,
The ash that looks like air.

Emerging, sailing,
Unrescuable grey-drenched browns
Of unpruned apple trees,
Their crush of twigs,
Threat of unleafed forks . . .

An apple is still stuck there,
Almost yellow in this light.
One survivor of harvest;
Unreachable,
It flourished but came to nothing.

Best efforts are negative,
Seriously beautiful, like art.
Clear light speaks valediction;
Sparse branches
In an orchard of goodbyes,

So many lines that spume or trail off
Beyond limits, their own reaches.
The sky is a net of black nerves,
Continued dream-lines of trees.
Fog's majesty,

Sheer strength of numbers, departs;
Swish of moth-eaten cloaks,
Coarse garments –
Generation upon labouring generation
Of conscripts and grocers' assistants,

Millhands, the unnamed courtiers
Of long-dead industrial magnates.
Their souls shine
On wet slates in summer, sliced turn
Of an autumn furrow, a now-sacred pippin,

As the snow melts like white grease
And soot-spotted stalactites vanish
In their own directions
To destinations that are sounds and wetness;
A soft, cold world
That grows dark when fog clears,
The ground that receives the apple.

In the Small Hotel

There they must live for ever, under soft lights,
The cheated at their favourite separate tables,
Inactive thirds of tender adulteries.

They stare into a light that is always evening,
Their eyes divided, as if distracted by
The ghost of something only one eye sees

Sleep-walking in plastic darkness
Around the night-clubs. They sit like chessmen
At their linen squares, waiting to be moved.

No one makes conversation. A hand
May absently arrange roses in a vase
Or wave away the leering gypsy fiddler.

Chefs please no one there and the waiters stamp
Untipped among customers too vague and lost
Ever to think of coming back to commerce.

People we did not want or could not keep;
Someone did this to them, over and over,
Wanting their unhappiness until it happened.

Across the dewy grass with a small suitcase
Love comes trotting and stops to hold on a shoe.
To go away with *her*! To drive the limousine

With contraceptives in the glove compartment
Beside the chocolates and packaged orchid
And find that new Arcadia replacing Hollywood! –

Remote and amatory, a style of life
In which no one offends or intrudes.
They might as well live in their wardrobes.

Unlucky Mariners

Clapped out, with long necks
And thin bodies pivoting
On paunches,
They sit like unstrung banjos
Waiting their names to be called.

I dream of rusting hulks
In the Indies,
Jammed among the mangrove
Where sea stops inch by inch,
Water, snakes and vegetable are one.

'John Rigg, you spilled your rum
From Stornoway to the dreary Plate.
I saw you wench Malacca
Under the palms;
You changed your ladies with the tide.'

Dance of the shingle resort,
Foreshore trash
And harbour-masters counting
Prosperity by tonnage –
Here are the makers of music,

The numbers missed by arithmetic,
Unshipped and down on their luck
As they have been down on their luck
In disgusting jails
Near all the harbours.

'MacBryde, you shipped out of Glasgow
In '32, and you're back
With five German duckings
And thoughts of as many bastards
As you've had slit-skirted slope-eyed whores.'

Once, on a raft on a lagoon
Of Renfrewshire's Clyde,
An old man waved from his freighter;
He had nothing to do but wave to me,
And I thought, 'I'll go to sea.'

I dream of rusting hulks
And undersea
The leaky tubs that God's torpedo
Plugged; in South Pacific huts
The lucky mariners, copra kings

With four wives and the respect
Of The Islands,
Playing much-repaired concertinas
Long into the night,
To the tropical stars.

And I look at this lot,
Calling out their names
From *The Ledger of Missing Seafarers*,
So seldom called
They think I call their fathers.

Their grey skins are radiant mist,
Their eyes deep pools
In which the monsters sleep –
From nautical boyhoods
To skeletal service on The Ghost Ship.

[51]

'Falkenberg, you've a lot
To answer for. Your slummy crew
Picked off the bobbing wrecks
Might answer to your bells
But you're shipless now.'

Wrecks of many seas,
Here by the silent shipyards
Of the shore, ghosts of nuts and bolts
Toast your epiphanies
In the transparent grave of the fish!

White Fields

An aeroplane, its red and green night-lights
Spotting its distant noise in the darkness;
'Jack Frost', you say, pointing to white fields
Sparkling. My eyes accept the dark, the fields
Extend, spreading and drifting, fences rising
Before the black hedge that zips beside the road
I'm told I must never try to cross without you.
'What time is it?' – 'The middle of the night!
You've had a dream, I heard you shout.'
It woke me and I cried aloud, until
My mother came and showed me the farm
Wasn't burning, the school still had its roof,
There was no one hidden in the little fir trees.
'Only an aeroplane!' – As if you meant
That there, in 1948 in Renfrewshire,
We were safe from fear, and the white eyes
Of dead Jews were just photographs
In a terrible past, a neighbour's magazine.
'Only an aeroplane!' Unsleeping factories,
All night you busied overhead, and flames
Flushed out my cities made of shoe-boxes
And dominoes, my native village of shaws.
Innocent machine! I had a toy like you
That I made buzz and drone like Leaper's bees,
From which I dropped the A-bomb on John's pram,
Crumpling the hand-embroidered sheets.

Our breath melted ice on the window-pane.
Fields drizzled on the glass, opening strips
Of short-lived clarity, and fingernails of ice
Slid to the sill. 'No harm will come to us.'
I slept. Till now I've slept, dreaming of mice
Burrowing under the crusted tufts of snow
That heaviest fall had left us with,
Our planet flooded into continents
Of stray, white islands, a sea too cold to swim.
Till now I've slept, and waking, I reject
Your generation, an old copy of *Everybody's*
Thrown out with *Film Fun* and the tea leaves,
Bulldozed by a conscript from our village
Into a pit dug by forced labour.
So easily is love shed, I hardly feel it.

    White fields, your angled frost filed sharply
Bright over undisturbed grasses, do not soothe
As similes of innocence or idle deaths
That must happen anyway, an unmoral blankness;
Be unforgiving stillness, natural, what is:
Crimes uttered in landscape, smoke-darkened snow.

    Trains in my distance altered. Cattle trucks
Seemed to chug through Georgetown, a station
Where a fat man in a black uniform kept hens
On the platform. The waggons sprouted arms
And dropped dung, and no one sang
'Ten Green Bottles' or 'The Sash.' Offensive outings.

Six years old! And I lived through the worst of it!

Clydesiders

Men in boiler-suits zip twice, Clyde-built.
Thirsts, you come to this, a gush against the Shanks,
Fag-ends in the urinal, Navy Cut
Of yellow leaf, little boats of Capstan
Along the trough, blue-bottles on a crust,
And down the drain, grey ash of smokers' silt.

My poems should be Clyde-built, crude and sure,
With images of those dole-deployed
To honour the indomitable Reds,
Clydesiders of slant steel and angled cranes;
A poetry of nuts and bolts, born, bred,
Embattled by the Clyde, tight and impure.

My footprints tread a rug of settled sawdust,
The carpentering corner of a Yard.
I made these marks, have gone back to London,
No victim of my place, but mad for it.
A shower of rain, my footprints melt and run.
They'll follow to my life. I know they must.

Caledonian Moonlight

The white moon opens over a ridge of bracken
Spilling its prodigal rays into the eyes
Of the last pair of wildcat in the county
Looking for the kittens of their sterility
In the wiry heather

And the beautiful white face of a secretary
Rises in the shut eyes of a bachelor caretaker
Whose mother is dreaming
Of handing a plate of sandwiches to the minister

There are more moons in the night
Than eyes of those who see them
Open, venereal

I Am a Cameraman

They suffer, and I catch only the surface.
The rest is inexpressible, beyond
What can be recorded. You can't be them.
If they'd talk to you, you might guess
What pain is like though they might spit on you.

Film is just a reflection
Of the matchless despair of the century.
There have been twenty centuries since charity began.
Indignation is day-to-day stuff;
It keeps us off the streets, it keeps us watching.

Film has no words of its own.
It is a silent waste of things happening
Without us, when it is too late to help.
What of the dignity of those caught suffering?
It hurts me. I robbed them of privacy.

My young friends think Film will be all of Art.
It will be revolutionary proof.
Their films will not guess wrongly and will not lie.
They'll film what is happening behind barbed wire.
They'll always know the truth and be famous.

Politics softens everything.
Truth is known only to its victims.
All else is photographs – a documentary
The starving and the playboys perish in.
Life disguises itself with professionalism.

Life tells the biggest lies of all,
And draws wages from itself.
Truth is a landscape the saintly tribes live on,
And all the lenses of Japan and Germany
Wouldn't know how to focus on it.

Life flickers on the frame like beautiful hummingbirds.
That is the film that always comes out blank.
The painting the artist can't get shapes to fit.
The poem that shrugs off every word you try.
The music no one has ever heard.

Restraint

It lives in the body,
Interior clothing
Woven under nakedness

On constant looms. Textile
Animal, it feeds on words,
Evasions that trick

What might have been
To what was never tried.
It laughs its head off

At funerals, is safe
And satisfied, the only
Creature ever satisfied.

A long course in freedom
Hurts it. It cries out
And makes you tell lies.

The Disguise

A funeral procession of barges
On industrial canals –
The nineteenth century, and last,
Celebrating itself, through counties
Ditched and bricked with its epitaphs.

History is illiterate.
It is 'effects', wars, 'conditions',
Boots at dawn and the closing of doors,
Ambition at its conferences.
Most live in an aftermath of its injustices.

And they say, 'Go out smiling, let your poems
Tickle the ribs of Optimism
On an absolute prosody that ticks over
With the strength of an intricate machine,
Not this free verse you can buy at Woolworths.'

But I *am* smiling, and against you.
There is an invective of grins, winks, fingers,
Up the sleeves of galactic offspring.
Through your trash go their impertinent smiles,
Hidden by glum masks, the finest insult.

from
Barbarians

'He was bored, but nevertheless he slowly grew
further and further away from the hardship and
simplicity of the workers, from his childhood
environment. He somehow learned how to behave, as
they say. Without realizing it, he cut himself off from
his own people. . . . He thought he was merely bored,
but secretly he was flattered at being included. Some
forces drew him towards the bourgeoisie; other forces
sought to retard his transition.'

'The truth of life was on the side of the men who
returned to their poor houses, on the side of the men
who had not "made good".'

Paul Nizan, *Antoine Bloyé*

The Come-on

'. . . the guardian, the king's son, who kept watch over the gates
of the garden in which I wanted to live.'

Albert Camus

To have watched the soul of my people
    Fingered by the callous
Enlivens the bitter ooze from my grudge.
    Mere seepage from 'background'
Takes over, blacking out what intellect
    Was nursed by school or book
Or had accrued by questioning the world.
    Enchanting, beloved texts
Searched in for a generous mandate for
    Believing who I am,
What I have lived and felt, might just as well
    Not exist when the vile
Come on with their 'coals in the bath' stories
    Or mock at your accent.
Even now I am an embarrassment
    To myself, my candour.
Listen now to the 'professional classes'
    Renewing claims to 'rights',
Possession of land, ownership of work,
    Decency of 'standards'.
In the bleep-bleep of versicles, leisure-novels,
    Black traffic of Oxbridge –
Books and bicycles, the bile of success –
    Men dressed in prunella
Utter credentials and their culture rules us,
    A culture of connivance,
Of 'authority', arts of bland recoveries.
    Where, then, is 'poetry'?

[63]

Brothers, they say that we have no culture.
    We are of the wrong world,
Our level is the popular, the media,
    The sensational columns,
Unless we enter through a narrow gate
    In a wall they have built
To join them in the 'disinterested tradition'
    Of tea, of couplets dipped
In sherry and the decanted, portentous remark.
    Therefore, we'll deafen them
With the dull staccato of our typewriters.
    But do not misbehave –
Threats and thrashings won't work: we're outnumbered.
    Drink ale if you must still,
But learn to tell one good wine from another –
    Our honesty is cunning.
We will beat them with decorum, with manners,
    As sly as language is.
Take tea with the king's son at the seminars –
    He won't know what's happening.
Carry your learning as does the mimic his face.
    Know one knife from another.
You will lose heart: don't show it. Be patient;
    And sit on that high wall
In its obstacle glass chips, its barbed wire,
    Watching the gardeners.
One day we will leap down, into the garden,
    And open the gate – *wide, wide.*
We too shall be kings' sons and guardians,
    And then there will be no wall:
Our grudges will look quaint and terrible.

In the Grounds

Yorkshire, 1975

Barbarians in a garden, softness does
Approve of who we are as it does those
Who when we speak proclaim us barbarous
And say we have no business with the rose.

Gently the grass waves, and its green applauds
The justice, not of progress, but of growth.
We walk as people on the paths of gods
And in our minds we harmonize them both.

Disclosures of these grounds – a river view,
Two Irish wolfhounds watching on a lawn;
A spinster with her sewing stares at you,
And begs you leave her pretty world alone.

More books than prejudice in our young minds . . .
We could not harm her, would not, would prefer
A noise less military and more kind
Than our boots make across her wide *parterre*.

We are intransigent, at odds with them.
They see our rabble-dreams as new contempt
For England's art of house and leaf. Condemn
Our clumsiness – you do not know, how, unkempt

And coarse, we hurt a truth with truth, still true
To who we are: barbarians, whose chins
Drool with ale-stinking hair, whose horses chew
Turf owned by watching, frightened mandarins,

Their surly nephews lounging at each gate,
Afraid we'll steal their family's treasured things,
Then hawk them – pictures, furniture and plate –
Round the encampments of our saddle-kings.

Here be Dragons
Pomponius Mela, *Chorographia*

In Africa, Pomponius Mela wrote,
Are tribes whose bodies stop below the throat.
His readers might not marvel much at that
Headless and monstrous proletariat
For Mela says that faces on their chests
Had all the usual features and, unless
Pomponius lied, I can suppose their art,
Doubtless oral, came straight from the heart.

There, too, in Africa, were troglodytes
Who housed themselves in the eternal night.
This Mela proffers civilized distaste.
He says of these non-citizens of waste
And downward-tunnelled tenements, they dined
On serpents they discovered as they mined.
But had they raised their tenements through sky,
What lunch would fowl-fed Mela specify?

Mela records a tribe that cursed the sun
At dusk and dawn. These people of No-One
Possessed no names and did not dream. Dreamless
Without nomenclature, did Mela bless
That dreamless people who knew more than he
Could ever know of their reality,
Cursing the sun, cursing at dusk and dawn,
For reasons Romans couldn't lay their fingers on?

These then were wonders Mela thought he saw
In lives reported as hair, skin and claw.
That flattered Rome, to keep its *regnum* sure –
The home of shave and soap and manicure.
One story's left, the one that Mela tells
That's their revenge – the one about the well.
Arriving there, thirsty and out of breath,
Romans might drink, then laugh themselves to death.

Gardeners

England, Loamshire, 1789
A gardener speaks, in the grounds of a great house,
to his Lordship

Gardens, gardens, and we are gardeners . . .
Razored hedgerow, flowers, those planted trees
Whose avenues conduct a greater ease
Of shadow to your own and ladies' skins
And tilt this Nature to magnificence
And natural delight. But pardon us,
My Lord, if we reluctantly admit
Our horticulture not the whole of it,
Forgetting, that for you, this elegance
Is not our work, but your far tidier Sense.

Out of humiliation comes that sweet
Humility that does no good. We know
Our coarser artistries will make things grow.
Others design the craftsmanship we fashion
To please your topographical possession.
A small humiliation – Yes, we eat,
Our crops and passions tucked out of the view
Across a shire, the name of which is you,
Where every native creature runs upon
Hills, moors and meadows which your named eyes own.

Our eyes are nameless, generally turned
Towards the earth our fingers sift all day –
Your day, your earth, your eyes, wearing away
Not earth, eyes, days, but scouring, forcing down
What lives in us and which you cannot own.
One of us heard the earth cry out. It spurned
His hands. It threw stones in his face. We found
That man, my Lord, and he was mad. We bound
His hands together and we heard him say –
'Not me! Not me who cries!' We took away

That man – remember, Lord? – and then we turned,
Hearing your steward order us return,
His oaths, and how you treated us with scorn.
They call this grudge. Let me hear you admit
That in the country that's but half of it.
Townsmen will wonder, when your house was burned,
We did not burn your gardens and undo
What likes of us did for the likes of you;
We did not raze this garden that we made,
Although we hanged you somewhere in its shade.

The Student

Of Renfrewshire, 1820

For our Mechanics' Literary Club
I study Tacitus. It takes all night
At this rough country table which I scrub
Before I sit at it, by candlelight,
Spreading my books on it. I think respect
Must work like love in any intellect.
    Difficult Latin sticks in my throat
    And the scarecrow wears my coat.

What put me up to it, this partnership
Of lexicon and text, these five books thieved,
These two books borrowed, handed down, this grip
Of mind on mind, this work? Am I deceived?
Is literature a life proved much too good
To have its place in our coarse neighbourhood?
    Difficult Latin sticks in my throat
    And the scarecrow wears my coat.

In Paisley when they read the Riot Act
We faced the horsemen of the 10th Hussars.
Men's bones were broken, angry heads were cracked –
Provosts, sheriffs, guns and iron bars.
We thrashed the poet William Motherwell,
That depute-sheriff and the law's law-minstrel.
    Difficult Latin sticks in my throat
    And the scarecrow wears my coat.

Between us and our lives were bayonets.
They shone like water. We were crooked with thirst,
That hot dry bubbling when your whole life sweats.
'If you want life', they said, 'you must die first.'
Thus in a drought of fear Republic died
On Linen Street, Lawn Street and Causeyside.
    Difficult Latin sticks in my throat
    And the scarecrow wears my coat.

Beneath our banners I was marching for
My scholarship of barley, secret work
On which authority must slam its door
As Rome on Goth, Byzantium on Turk.
I'm left to guess their books, which precious line,
Eluding me, is never to be mine.
    Difficult Latin sticks in my throat
    And the scarecrow wears my coat.

Frost, poverty, rare, rare, the rapid rain . . .
What good can come of study, I must have.
I read it once, then read it twice again.
Fox, whittrick, dog, my horse, my new-born calf –
Let me recite my life, my animals and clay,
My candlelight, my fuddled melody.
    Difficult Latin sticks in my throat
    And the scarecrow wears my coat.

Such hard work urges me to turn each line
As firmly as I plough a furrow straight,
By doing so make this work clandestine,
Mix its affections with both love and hate.
So, Tacitus, old friend, though not to me,
Allow me master your authority.
    Difficult Latin sticks in my throat
    And the scarecrow wears my coat.

[72]

Empires

All the dead Imperia . . . They have gone
Taking their atlases and grand pianos.
They could not leave geography alone.
They conquered with the thistle and the rose.
To our forefathers it was right to raise
Their pretty flag at every foreign dawn
Then lower it at sunset in a haze
Of bugle-brass. They interfered with place,
Time, people, lives, and so to bed. They died
When it died. It had died before. It died
Before they did. They did not know it. Race,
Power, Trade, Fleet, a hundred regiments,
Postponed that final reckoning with pride,
Which was expensive. Counting up the cost
We plunder morals from the power they lost.
They ruined us. They conquered continents.
We filled their uniforms. We cruised the seas.
We worked their mines and made their histories.
You work, we rule, they said. We worked; they ruled.
They fooled the tenements. All men were fooled.
It still persists. It will be so, always.
Listen. An out-of-work apprentice plays
God Save the Queen on an Edwardian flute.
He is, but does not know it, destitute.

The Wealth

When he returned to New York in December 1965, he
figured his stay would be a brief one, that he'd earn
$25,000 if he was lucky, enough to live comfortably in
England. Instead, he earned ten times that much.
The success – and the terrors that accompanied it –
had begun.

Paul Cowan, on Paul Simon
Rolling Stone, 1 July, 1976

If I prove nothing to you, it's my fault.
The planet's round and greedy.
This song-infatuated globe can't handle it,
In love with rip-off and reward.

It is an old perdition to be rich,
An old displeasure to be seen dismayed
With what you wanted, when, having it, it hurts
Or turns against you in the night.

The last day of December '65
I got a letter from your Uncle Sam.
I'd thought of him as one of the good guys,
Stern, dressed in a dollar, but on our side.

By then I was in two minds.
A lot of people were dying, like clichés.
I wasn't even an American.
Gabe read my papers over, then we hit the town.

The Go-Go girls brought New Year in
Dancing on our table – *Sloopy, hang on!*
I didn't lose my mind in drink. I sulked.
The night-club scooped me up and took me home.

I walked to the bus depot in the snow.
January. They took us to Cleveland.
I didn't want to go. Nick said, 'Go. Buy time.'
We walked around, afraid in underpants.

Faced with a form, I opted for the Coastguard,
'And don't let me see any damn fool
Write "coastguard", gentlemen,' yelled a sailor.
There were six-foot-six football giants

Who fainted away in the lottery
Of the blood-test. I wouldn't have missed it,
Not for anything. I didn't faint. I felt –
I felt *proud*. And then *I* couldn't pee in the cup.

A doctor said, if he was me, he'd go back
To Scotland. 'Randall Jarrell,' I said.
The man next in line pushed me, and asked
If I was 'some kinda coward'. 'Yes,' I said.

I said I wasn't an American.
You can't say that to a man in blue jockey-shorts
Who'd been insisting on the Marine Corps.
'A medical is close enough,' I said.

If that man went to Vietnam, I hope
He didn't die, or kill anyone,
Or help reduce thin children to
An orphanage of ash.

We used to visit in Peninsula, Ohio,
A precious farmhouse on a wooded hill.
I planted corn, walked on an Indian trail,
James Fenimore Cooper for a day.

[75]

The poems in my head were facing west
Towards a continental summer.
I won't deny it. The Stars and Stripes
On a blue autumn day is quite something.

But then, so was I, in casuals,
Fit and young, athletic, frivolous –
As if nobody knew me then – one round year married,
My wife in tears at having to go home so soon.

I liked old villages with soldier-statued squares
Where I could stand and feel like Robert Lowell.
Still there, and probably the same,
Each with its radical son and its casualty.

States of long trains and the astounding autumn,
I squeaked before your laws, reduced
To nakedness, my penis in a cup
Refusing Uncle Sam his specimen of me –

My health, portrayed in Akron's
Tax-paid chemicals, *Cutty Sark*,
Upper New York State wine – oh, Liz, *your* wine! –
And food bought in the Kroger Store.

We shipped aboard SS *United States*.
I went home on a name
With nothing like enough
To live on comfortably.

I felt like a Jew, at Hamburg
On a boat bound for America,
A Jew at Hamburg, 1939,
And wept for laws, but not for me, civilian,

Writing poetry, seasick on the North Atlantic,
Reading *Henderson the Rain King*
And *For the Union Dead*.
I wanted it torpedoed, by the British.

But, for you, a terror was beginning . . .
Such is the magnitude of song.
An American critic, writing of
An English poet who thinks himself classical,

Has said of tenderness, it is
'The social face of self-pity'.
If I say, tenderly, I am afraid,
Who do I fear, or what? *Horror.* 'The wealth! The wealth!'

America, I admit it. You've beaten me.
I'll end up in a regiment of *foederati*
To be led for ever by a minor Belisarius
Against my kin in the forests of Europe.

Our armoured herds are grazing on the map.
And so are theirs. I write this for *détente*,
Which, as ever, should be personal.
One false move then, I'd have no right to speak.

In your culture, I am a barbarian,
But I'm that here, and everywhere,
Lulled by alien rites, lullabyed with remorse
Here on the backstreets of the universe.

Elegy for the Lost Parish

Dream, ploughman, of what agriculture brings,
Your eggs, your bacon to your greasy plate;
Then listen to the evening's thrush that sings
Exhilarated sadness and the intimate.

Your son's in Canada, growing his wheat
On fields the size of farms, and prosperous
On grain and granary. His world's replete
With life and love and house and happiness.

Dream, ploughman, of the lovely girl who died
So many summers gone, whose face will come
To you, call to you, and be deified
In sunlight on one cut chrysanthemum.

A nod of nettles flutters its green dust
Across small fields where you have mown the hay.
So wipe your brow, as on a scented gust
Your past flies in and will not go away.

Dream, ploughman, of old characters you've known
Who taught you things of scythe and horse and plough;
Of fields prepared, seed rhythmically sown,
Their ways of work that are forgotten now.

Remember, sir, and let them come to you
Out of your eye to mutter requiem,
Praising fidelities, the good of you.
Allow their consolations, cherish them

Into a privacy, as, with hand's slow shake
You reach towards your glass, your hands reach to
Where no one is or can be. Heartbreak,
Heartbreak and loneliness of virtue.

Watches of Grandfathers

They go with corporations
And with fountain pens,
With honour and inscription,
Fastidious longevities
In which are reckoned
The funerals of friends.

Worn in relation to work,
Timetables, opening times,
And counterparts carried by
Despicable referees,
They are neat in the palm of a hand.
Always to be dangled before

Babies in prams, consulted
With flourishes that invite
Benevolent side-glances,
They have a kindness
Which the artistry of time
In its steady circles

Denies, as it measures
Proximity to pensionable age,
Or, from a safe hook
In the corner of a workshop,
Hung there, stare at the bench
As they mutter 'Death, Death'.

They long for the pocket
Of the eldest son, in
The waistcoat he will buy for one,
Who will see his father's eye
Glazed on it, and the age
Of his sons slowly numbered.

Portrait Photograph, 1915

We too have our place, who were not photographed
So much and then only in multitudes
Rising from holes in the ground to fall into smoke
Or is it newsreel beyond newsreel
But I do not know and I have lost my name
And my face and as for dignity
I never had it in any case, except once,
I think, in the High Street, before we left
For troopships and the farewell pipers,
When it was my turn in the queue
In Anderson's Photographic Arcade and Salon,
In my uniform, and I was not a tall man
Although for a moment I had a sense
Of posterity in the eyes of descendants,
Of my own face in a frame on a small table
Over which her eyes would go, and my sons',
And that I would persist, in day and night,
Fading a little as they say they do.

Drowning

Why give the place its name, when it has changed,
Where, in the grasping waters of the Gryfe,
He, his name forgotten now, was drowned?
What is remembered is his little life.

Ask any man of forty-odd or so,
He'd think a bit, as if he had to try
To bring that name back from its tragedy,
Though, struggling with the tide, he saw him die.

One I could ask was wild, swam in the buff
Where Gryfe's clean waters raced the greedy Clyde
Beside that bridge where ladies parked and watched.
To dry himself, he ran the countryside.

Kirk elder now, who shot the sparrows down
With airgun resting on a garden fence,
How fares your soul, handing out the hymnals,
Who in your sin worked wicked innocence?

One I could ask has crossed the Scottish seas.
From Canada, we've heard no news at all.
He took his boots, his two sly winger's feet.
We miss that man as if he'd pinched our ball.

Most stayed at home, or near it, so they drink
On Friday nights or Saturdays and where
Men know each other and suppress remarks
On sagging bellies or receding hair.

One I could ask has fired his life away
With bottle after bottle to his mouth,
Raw liquor in the turpitude of ditches
While blubbering a sermon on his youth.

Ask any man of forty-odd or so
Around that parish by the Clyde's run sweat,
He'll shake his head as if he has forgotten,
Then walk away, and wish he could forget.

Remember, how we ran up to the bank
And, naked, how we screamed and jumped right in?
Those ladies, watching, must have thought we tried
To please them with a courtesy of skin.

That was our time, and after he was drowned.
It did not mean we had forgotten him.
It is a law, to disobey scared parents.
What better pool than his in which to swim?

But watch the changing waters, when the tide
Runs up, its shoulders hunched, with winking eyes,
And with a nip of sea and a dark surface
It steals the calm reflection from the sky.

They worked him free. They packed his clothes around
    him.
They sat him on his bike and wheeled him home.
Too young for swimming then, I was in goal,
When, from our pitch, I saw the dead boys come.

Ballad of the Two Left Hands

When walking out one morning
    Walking down Clydeside Street
I met a man with two left hands
    Who said he was obsolete.

At noon the work horns sounded through
    The shipyards on Clyde's shore
And told men that the day had come
    When they'd work there no more.

Economy is hand and sweat
    A welder in his mask
A new apprentice pouring tea
    From his father's thermos flask.

And soon these men of several trades
    Stood there on Clydeside Street
Stood staring at each new left hand
    That made them obsolete.

'Beware of men in suits,' one said
    'Take it from me, it's true
Their drivel economics'll
    Put two left hands on you.'

All in the afternoon was shut
    When I walked out again
The day had pulled on its black gloves
    And turned its back on men.

[85]

I walked the dusk of darkened cranes
  Clyde broke on Clyde's dark shore
And rivets fired where men still work
  Though men work here no more.

High in the night's dark universe
  I saw the promised star
That men I knew raise glasses to
  In an illegal bar.

They toast that city still to come
  Where truth and justice meet
And though they don't know where it is
  It's not on Clydeside Street.

With thumbs stuck on the wrong way round
  In two left-footed shoes
I saw a man search in his heart
  And ask it, 'Are you true?'

That man who sat on Clydeside Street
  Looked up at me and said
'I'll study this, then I'll pick clean
  The insides of my head.'

And moonlight washed the shipyards then
  Each crane was hung with stars
Rinsed in the moonlight we stared up
  Like old astronomers.

Economy is hand and sweat
  And foundrymen and fire
Revise your textbooks, multiply
  Your guilt by your desire.

Such dignity, so many lives,
Even on Clydeside Street
When mind and heart together ask
'Why are we obsolete?'

Lost Gloves

I leave my body in a new blue suit
  With my soul, which is newly destitute.
Rinsed spirit of me, washed for this departure,
  Takes off adroitly to its atmosphere.

And here's that blue glove on a railing's tip
  Where iron, frost and wool make partnership
Of animal and elements and blue –
  Lost little glove, I still remember you.

You do not fit my hand now, nor can I fit
  My world with life; nor my mouth match its spit;
My tongue, my words; my eyes, the things they see.
  My head is upside down in memory.

A child walks to his mother, right hand bare
  And hidden in his coat, then follows her
Inside, his gloved hand on the banister,
  His right hand on his heart, remaining there.

My pulse beats backwards to a street in winter –
  Blue first perceived, that I now disinter
Blue out of blue where life and childhood crossed:
  Five blue wool-fingers waving in the frost.

Stranger's Grief

i.m. Robert Lowell

It's as if I've grown old, sitting like this
In a small park by the Lot in Cahors
Where autumn is arriving through its mist
To surprise my life with its metaphor.

In an *Observer*, four days out of date,
I've read the poet Lowell's dead. . . . New York,
New York, where smoke and whisky concentrate
Their traffic, architecture, art and work.

Across this river which is brown and fast
There is a paddock boys are running round,
Each one determined not to finish last.
Breath from their mouths drags after them like sound.

That's where the summer stops and autumn starts.
A gentle cadence in the wind will sing
Natural elegies, its counterparts
Of human sadness drowned in everything.

Youth's country is impossibly across
A wide river. How anyone can come
From there, and not look back, or feel no loss,
Always amazes me. I call youth *home*;

I'd go back if I could. I don't feel warmed
By death. To die is nothing very grand.
This world is delicate and misinformed.
It's growing old I've failed to understand.

What else can I do, feeling this way, but sit
With my wife and my newspaper, well-fed,
Well-wined, happy together and unfit.
Is it a happiness like this, being dead?

A radio, its non-specific song
Far away in a leafy park . . . I'm full
Of my routine sadness. It can't be wrong
To let these thoughts run free and overrule

Tranquillity, absorbing time and place,
And what I've read, and you and me, each half
Of this one silent couple, face to face,
As still as lovers in a lithograph.

It is like waiting, learning how to die,
Opened to sweetness, neutral as a leaf
Watching leaves falling. Notice how they lie,
How each survivor shares each stranger's grief.

On Her Picture Left with Him

On trains to London and the south
    And thus away from me
These words in my enamoured mouth
    Summon the flattery
Of who it is and what I love,
    Distracting me.

Lady, so far outside, and gone,
    Your picture left with me
Is like the world I look upon
    And shows reality
As who it is and why I love,
    Distracting me.

Thus do I gaze on you, and drink
    Your face you left with me,
And speak to you in whispered ink
    With that humility
Which is a lesser spoil of love,
    Distracting me.

Now is the afternoon turned round
    To dusk that darkens me,
And walking on nocturnal ground
    Offers no liberty
From who I am and who I love,
    Distracting me.

from
St Kilda's Parliament

In Memoriam
William Douglas Dunn
1911–1980

St Kilda's Parliament: 1879–1979

The photographer revisits his picture

On either side of a rock-paved lane,
Two files of men are standing barefooted,
Bearded, waistcoated, each with a tam-o'-shanter
On his head, and most with a set half-smile
That comes from their companionship with rock,
With soft mists, with rain, with roaring gales,
And from a diet of solan goose and eggs,
A diet of dulse and sloke and sea-tangle,
And ignorance of what a pig, a bee, a rat,
Or rabbit look like, although they remember
The three apples brought here by a traveller
Five years ago, and have discussed them since.
And there are several dogs doing nothing
Who seem contemptuous of my camera,
And a woman who might not believe it
If she were told of the populous mainland.
A man sits on a bank by the door of his house,
Staring out to sea and at a small craft
Bobbing there, the little boat that brought me here,
Whose carpentry was slowly shaped by waves,
By a history of these northern waters.
Wise men or simpletons – it is hard to tell –
But in that way they almost look alike
You also see how each is individual,
Proud of his shyness and of his small life
On this outcast of the Hebrides
With his eyes full of weather and seabirds,
Fish, and whatever morsel he grows here.
Clear, too, is manhood, and how each man looks
Secure in the love of a woman who
Also knows the wisdom of the sun rising,

Of weather in the eyes like landmarks.
Fifty years before depopulation –
Before the boats came at their own request
To ease them from their dying babies –
It was easy, even then, to imagine
St Kilda return to its naked self,
Its archaeology of hazelraw
And footprints stratified beneath the lichen.
See, how simple it all is, these toes
Playfully clutching the edge of a boulder.
It is a remote democracy, where men,
In manacles of place, outstare a sea
That rattes back its manacles of salt,
The moody jailer of the wild Atlantic.
　　　Traveller, tourist with your mind set on
Romantic Staffas and materials for
Winter conversations, if you should go there,
Landing at sunrise on its difficult shores,
On St Kilda you will surely hear Gaelic
Spoken softly like a poetry of ghosts
By those who never were contorted by
Hierarchies of cuisine and literacy.
You need only look at the faces of these men
Standing there like everybody's ancestors,
This flick of time I shuttered on a face.
Look at their sly, assuring mockery.
They are aware of what we are up to
With our internal explorations, our
Designs of affluence and education.
They know us so well, and are not jealous,
Whose be-all and end-all was an eternal
Casual husbandry upon a toehold
Of Europe, which, when failing, was not their fault.
You can see they have already prophesied
A day when survivors look across the stern

Of a departing vessel for the last time
At their gannet-shrouded cliffs, and the farewells
Of the St Kilda mouse and St Kilda wren
As they fall into the texts of specialists,
Ornithological visitors at the prow
Of a sullenly managed boat from the future.
They pose for ever outside their parliament,
Looking at me, as if they have grown from
Affection scattered across my own eyes.
And it is because of this that I, who took
This photograph in a year of many events –
The Zulu massacres, Tchaikovsky's opera –
Return to tell you this, and that after
My many photographs of distressed cities,
My portraits of successive elegants,
Of the emaciated dead, the lost empires,
Exploded fleets, and of the writhing flesh
Of dead civilians and commercial copulations,
That after so much of that larger franchise
It is to this island that I return.
Here I whittle time, like a dry stick,
From sunrise to sunset, among the groans
And sighings of a tongue I cannot speak,
Outside a parliament, looking at them,
As they, too, must always look at me
Looking through my apparatus at them
Looking. Benevolent, or malign? But who,
At this late stage, could tell, or think it worth it?
For I was there, and am, and I forget.

The Apple Tree

'And if the world should end tomorrow,
I still would plant my apple tree.'

Luther

I could play the bad eras like a concertina.
Multiple chords would squeak like 'Excuse me',
'I beg your pardon', 'Oops' and 'Sorry, no thank you.'
Pump hard on a squeeze-box and you can almost hear
The Protestant clerks of northern Europe in Hell,
Complaisant men who filed the paperwork of death
Or signed the warrants, exemplary in private life
But puritanical before their desks of duty.
Say what you like, their Gods did not approve of them.

Men moaned of Scotland that its barren air and soil
Couldn't so much as ripen an apple. I can hear
Their croaked whispers reproach the stern and wild of
  Alba,
Naming our Kirk, our character, our coarse consent
To drunken decency and sober violence,
Our paradox of ways. Here, in the lovely land,
Beside Kirkmaiden, enumerating apple trees,
I feel the simple millions groan, 'Keep you your faith.
A sapling nursed to fruit impersonates salvation.'

Kirk-sanctioned crimes, Kirk-flourished trade, Kirk-coded
  commerce –
Say what you like, our Gods have not approved of them
While apples ripen round the mist-mild farms and
  gardens.
Good nature and a scent of fruit at dailygone
Make more of our acceptances and affirmations
Than quick links forced from character to climate.
Name you our beasts and trees, our rivers raced with fish,
Our islands, oceans, mountains and our field-sweet crops.
These too define a people named in city stone.

Four horses chew among the windfalls. Fallen fruits
Spill sweetening juices on the orchard grass, frosted
Into their leaking bruises and hoofed into pulp.
Last wasps grow fat and a tantrum of stings threatens
The man on his ladder, who cups an apple in
The stretch of his hand, then plucks it down, to bite
Its greeny red, rubbed on his overalls. He stands
Up there, eating an apple among all the apples
While big mares and their foals munch on the apple-grass.

At night the orchard is a brew of leaf and fruit,
Feeling the pinch of autumn. Spread sneddins release
The sounds that lie in wait in wood, and over there
An upland wilderness reposes in chilled beauty.
Burns spate with cleanliness of rain, that clean high
  ground
Carrion crow and left-alone mountain sheep administer.
Crag-country, wet and wiry, but fertile to the eye;
A lung-and-heart testing land, but by a ruin there
You will find crab-apple trees, black harp-strings in the
  wind.

Tonight I saw the stars trapped underneath the water.
I signed the simple covenant we keep with love.
One hand held out an apple while the other held
Earth from a kirkyard where the dead remember me.
In these lost hollows of the stern conventicles
A faith is kept with land and fruit. Already are
New scriptures written by the late-arriving autumn,
That postponed shuffle of leaves, that white frost-writing.
These are my missionary fruits, a kindred taste.

Then let my Gods be miracles brought on stone boats
By Conval and the first dailyday folk before him.
Rather an ordinary joy – a girl with a basket,
With apples under a linen cloth – than comfortless
With windlestrae to eat. Forge no false links of man
To land or creed, the true are good enough. Our lives
Crave codes of courtesy, ways of describing love,
And these, in a good-natured land, are ways to weep,
True comfort as you wipe your eyes and try to live.

An Address on the Destitution of Scotland

Who would have thought it, and not me, not me,
That a boy who shawed turnips with a large gully
By the side of Cousar's cart and snort-breathed
   Clydesdale,
Who worked in the blue-and-red darkening dusk of
   childhood,
Would grow into this archivist of Red desires?
Far away are the chills of original Octobers.
My eyes are heavy now with alien perspectives,
And I am sick of the decisions of philosophers –
Dirty hands, dirty hands of turncoats and opinion-makers.
It was a long road back to this undeclared Republic.
I came by the by-ways, empty of milestones,
On the roads of old drovers, by disused workings.

So here I am, returned to your shabby encampments.
I, too, have scrounged on open fields, ripped up
Into their gathering of released good stinks
That mingle in the first-few-hours-of-shaws-rotting,
That reek of roots, that tactile, lunatic aroma
Tasting of dialect and curses sent out to work.
Tell me of your tinkerdom, of this poverty
Among you, raddled by a destitute polity,
The fields abandoned to old supermarket trolleys,
An ancient soot, the Clyde returning to its nature.
On which blasphemy do you blame your outcast silence,
Bedraggled here with your billy-cans and supper?

Share with me, then, the sad glugs in your bottles;
Throw a stolen spud for me on the side-embers.
Allow me to pull up a brick, and to sit beside you
In this nocturne of modernity, to speak of the dead,
Of the creatures loping from their dens of extinction.
Who are you waiting for? The stern mountain-preacher
In his coat of biblical night? I have seen him.
He sleeps in a kiln, out of the way of dragoons;
And I met a subversive optimist, at Sanquhar.
Permit me, then, to join your circle around your fire
In this midden of warm faces and freezing backs.
Sing me your songs in the speech of timber and horse.

Witch-girl

For evermore, they said, that girl was lame
In hands and feet, and that, they said, was proof
The lightless Devil spelled her into horse,
Moulding her hands and feet in solid hoof.

Poor girl, her mother saddled her, then rode
Through Sutherland until the outraged Law
Attended to the giddy-ups of gossip,
Force-feeding both of them on Tolbooth straw.

Only her mother was condemned. A pious mob –
Citizens and presbyters – whinnied, neighed,
Clip-clopped, as, standing in their fear of God,
There too were men who watched but also pitied.

Cold day in Dornoch . . . Shivering, the witch
Relieved her freezing round that fire which burned
To burn her up. Crowds psalmed with horror.
She blistered in the tar and, screaming, burned.

They spoke in Dornoch how the horses mourned
And how that lame girl, wandering, was heard
Tearing at the grass; and how she sat and sang,
As if the Devil also made her bird;

And how she washed her lameness in the rivers
From Oykell to the Clyde and Tweed and Forth,
Notorious as something to be pitied,
A girl to look at but a beast in worth.

No one could see her but would think he saw
Hoof in her fumbling hands, her staggering gait.
They spurned her flowers, as if they'd grown from her;
They barbed their righteous charity with hate.

She hawked her flowers in Glasgow, by the Trongate;
In Edinburgh, selling flowers, she slept
Beside the braziers of the City Guard.
The earth and animals within her wept.

No one to help her; no one saw her die,
If she is dead. By Gryfe, by Deveron,
By Cree and Tay, I see her wash her lameness,
And hear her breathing in the wood and stone.

Washing the Coins

You'd start at seven, and then you'd bend your back
Until they let you stand up straight, your hands
Pressed on your kidneys as you groaned for lunch,
Thick sandwiches in grease-proofed bundles, piled
Beside the jackets by the hawthorn hedges.
And then you'd bend your little back again
Until they let you stand up straight. Your hands,
On which the earth had dried in layers, itched, itched,
Though worse still was that ache along the tips
Of every picking finger, each broken nail
That scraped the ground for sprawled potatoes
The turning digger churned out of the drills.
Muttering strong Irish men and women worked
Quicker than local boys. You had to watch them.
They had the trick of sideways-bolted spuds
Fast to your ear, and the upset wire basket
That broke your heart but made the Irish laugh.
You moaned, complained, and learned the rules of work.
Your boots, enlarging as the day wore on,
Were weighted by the magnets of the earth,
And rain in the face was also to have
Something in common with bedraggled Irish.
You held your hands into the rain, then watched
Brown water drip along your chilling fingers
Until you saw the colour of your skin
Through rips disfiguring your gloves of mud.
It was the same for everyone. All day
That bead of sweat tickled your smeared nose
And a glance upwards would show you trees and clouds
In turbulent collusions of the sky
With ground and ground with sky, and you portrayed
Among the wretched of the native earth.

[105]

Towards the end you felt you understood
The happy rancour of the Irish howkers.
When dusk came down, you stood beside the byre
For the farmer's wife to pay the labour off.
And this is what I remember by the dark
Whitewash of the byre wall among shuffling boots.
She knew me, but she couldn't tell my face
From an Irish boy's, and she apologized
And roughed my hair as into my cupped hands
She poured a dozen pennies of the realm
And placed two florins there, then cupped her hands
Around my hands, like praying together.
It is not good to feel you have no future.
My clotted hands turned coins to muddy copper.
I tumbled all my coins upon our table.
My mother ran a basin of hot water.
We bathed my wages and we scrubbed them clean.
Once all that sediment was washed away,
That residue of field caked on my money,
I filled the basin to its brim with cold;
And when the water settled I could see
Two English kings among their drowned Britannias.

Galloway Motor Farm

They spoil a farm, already written off
Against experience or income tax –
Two Land Rovers, several tractors,
These wooden cattle-floats like shanty huts;
A Jaguar, garaged in the air and grass,
On highways of self-heal and lady's bedstraw;
A Morris shooting-brake is bedded down
With agricultural gear and tackle.

Scattered beside derelict byres and barns,
Awkward, out of place, they lie here, eyesores
Cast out from progress, maladroitly banned
Machinery, discarded implements.
Wastrel existences, I can hear them
As each one wrestles free of function,
Picked over, plundered by who dumped them here,
Already scavenged for their feus of scrap.

The chemistry of weather has installed
Its scaffolding, from which it builds its rusts
On the iron of a horse-drawn reaper.
Air braces itself before stinging nettles.
Car doors, bumpers, bonnets, mudguards, engines –
Earth will not have them back until their steels,
Their chromes, veneers and leathers marry with
These stony contours as the brides of place.

[107]

I will be glad to have been here, living
Within this stung bubble where antiquities
Freshen, where they breathe the present tense.
Docken, yarrow, the muscular turf, ignore
These rubbished profits and spent wages.
It all means less than nothing to the bat
On his manic itinerary, and the fox
Was born too late to live with other landmarks.

As for a man, then he may walk beside
These thumbed-down vehicles, posing the moon
Against the window of a truck's high cabin;
Or sit inside, behind the wheel, thinking
A roadless countryside as he pretends
He's motoring through the night. Scotland, come back
From the lost ground of your dismantled lands.
A carelessness has defaced even the bluebell.

Tonight, by a steading, an iron reaper
That once outscythed the scythe
Is a silent cry of its materials,
With all its blunt blades yearning for the stone.
It has come from the yonside of invention,
From pulverable ore and foundry hammers.
Old harness rots above the rusted horseshoes.
Unborn horses graze on the back pastures.

The Harp of Renfrewshire
Contemplating a map

Annals of the trilled R, gently stroked L,
Lamenting O of local literature,
Open, on this, their one-page book, a still
Land-language chattered in a river's burr.

Small-talk of herdsmen, rural argument –
These soft disputes drift over river-meadows,
A darg of conversations, a verbal scent –
Tut-tutted discourse, time of day, word-brose.

Named places have been dictionaried in
Ground's secret lexicon, its racial moan
Of etymology and cries of pain
That slit a summer wind and then were gone.

A mother calls her daughter from her door.
Her house, my stone illusion, hugs its hill.
From Eaglesham west to the rocky shore
Her cry is stretched across bog-asphodel.

The patronymic miles of grass and weddings,
Their festivals of gender, covenants,
Poor pre-industrially scattered steadings,
Ploughed-up davochs – old names, inhabitants.

And on my map is neither wall or fence,
But men and women and their revenue,
As, watching them, I utter into silence
A granary of whispers rinsed in dew.

Rose

So, little rose, it is all over
And you need no longer
Explore your cupped shapes,
Your fine organic enamels.

Four days you sat there
In a simple blue glass.
I watched you, I watched you;
I kept my eye on you.

My love is four days gone from me.
You have been good company.
I knew it would be like this –
You'd die the day of her return.

You have sat there in silence
Like a thought prayer.
You have been my good intentions.
You listened to me with patience.

Now I am in a gentle panic,
Not knowing what to do with you.
I will make up a ritual
For the departures of roses.

You will go into the heaven
Of unforgotten things.
Matisse will paint you;
Or Samuel Peploe will.

The door of her taxi is closing.
But you did not tell me your secrets.
I shall drink the water
Which did not preserve you long enough.

I will remember you in the French language.
I eat you now to keep you for ever.
Hello, my love. See?
This thorn has cut my lips.

Saturday

For Sandra and Chetwyn

Driving along the B1248
We pass such villages as Wetwang, or
North Grimston of descending Z-bends.
The Wolds are rolling for our benefit;
The long woods stride towards the eastern shore.
Frost sparks refrigerated ploughland to
A fan of silver ribs, good husbandry
In straight lines, going downhill to a point,
A misted earthen star, half-frost, half-ground.
And we are going to our country friends
At Kirkbymoorside, bearing a pineapple,
Some books of interest and a fine Bordeaux.
I wish it to be today, always, one hour
On this, the pleasant side of history.

Courting

On a summer's night to come
We'll find ourselves walking
Through a familiar Park.
I feel it happening –
Surprised anachronisms
In a delight, posed as
Hand-holding listeners to
Light overtures, percussed
From a lanterned bandstand
Through shaken foliage.

An autumn afternoon
Rehearses mist and brown
For a rediscovery –
That colour of angels
Flighted with chestnut leaves
Above the arrogant
Scarf-tightening waterfall,
A down-roar of water
Into the sinister
Conventional shadows.

It is already chosen,
A retrospective Sunday
When the still lake is glazed,
When bird-bread breaks underfoot,
Frost-toasted on cinder paths
And rhododendrons look
Snowed green exotica,
A botany of drips:
We will walk there again
With our white conversations.

Gardened from countryside,
The Park heaps love-days
On nature's edge; it is
An album of the Spring
In that season: woodland's
Municipal surprise,
Vernal formalities,
Mute orchestras of bluebells
When light leans on the leaf
And the thrush sings of rain.

Come with me now, dear girl,
And we will walk our years
Together. They open,
As gates do, or books, the heart's
Preliminary landmarks –
That path that leads nowhere
And a meadow beyond;
This path that leads into
Wilder greens of love,
A grass for walking on.

Second-hand Clothes

A girl anoints a dress
With four silver coins.
Hands rinse among textiles,
Encountering others' skins.
Held up, observed for rips,
For their proximities
To new, to cleanliness,
To fit, their owners are
A hearsay of shapes, a bag
At these elbows, a button
Gone from this tight collar.
I think of all the feet
That walked in these shoes,
Toes down-pointing now from
A rail, each rail-held heel,
And each scuffed toe, caught in
The second-hand quadrille.
The strict proprietrix
Flicks ash on the bare floor.
The boards are a brushed dirt.
Even these women look
As taken off as shirts,
Worn sweaters, skirts, sea-boots,
And thrown down on a floor.
Coats, ranked on their hangers,
Pose – shamed vagrants, slaves
Whose prices she calls out
As you shuffle their shrugs.
And here a man may buy
One cufflink, scarves, or socks,
A glove, or soup-stained tie,
Or a large box of dust.

There could have been a war
Yesterday. I walk home,
A suitably ashamed
Observer of the poor;
And I wonder at the coins
On her watery tray,
By her pot-plants. What does
She wish for, having stood
So long by the red bars
Of her electric fire
In her shop, having seen
The fact of poverty
And served its enterprise
In England, arms folded,
Witnessing its shame,
Its sizes, dignity,
The hard, proud faces of
Regular customers,
Who buy, sell, delve into
Her tubs of washed-out thread?
A shabby drunk goes down
In a corner puddle.
When I got home, I crawled
Into my mouth, sat down,
And fell into a cloth sleep.
There's nothing to be done
Save follow the lost shoes.

Remembering Lunch

Noticing from what they talk about, and how they stand, or
  walk,
That my friends have lost the ability or inclination to wander
Along the shores of an estuary or sea in contented solitude,
Disturbs me on the increasingly tedious subject of myself.
I long for more chances to walk along depopulated shores,
For more hours dedicated to fine discriminations of mud
As it shades from grey to silver or dries into soft pottery;
Discriminations of wind, sky, rough grasses and
  water-birds,
And, above all, to be well-dressed in tweeds and serviceable
  shoes
Although not like an inverted popinjay of the demented
  gentry
But as a schoolmaster of some reading and sensibility
Circa 1930 and up to his eccentric week-end pursuits,
  noticing,
Before the flood of specialists, the trace of lost peoples
In a partly eroded mound, marks in the earth, or this and that
Turned over with the aforementioned impermeable
  footwear.
Describing this to my strangely sophisticated companions
Is to observe them docket it for future reference in
A pigeon-hole of the mind labelled *Possible Satires*.
We are far gone in our own decay. I admit it freely,
Longing no more for even the wherewithal of decent
  sufficiency
Or whatever hypothetical brilliance makes it possible.
Whatever my friends long for, they no longer confess it
In the afternoon twilight of a long lunch in London
After that moment when the last carafe has been ordered.
Such delicate conversations of years gone by! You would
  think

[117]

Perceptions of this sort best left for approaching senility,
Especially as, in my case, I was not born ever to expect
To enjoy so long-drawn-out a lunchtime at steep prices
Among tolerant waiters resigned to our lasting presences
As if they sense a recapitulation by young men of young
men
In that fine hour of Edwardian promise at the *Tour Eiffel*
Or expatriate Americans and Irishmen in 'twenties Paris.
It is pretty well standard among literary phenomena.
Whether in the Rome of Marcus Martialis or London
ordinaries
Favoured by roaring playwrights and poets destined for
Future righteousness or a destructive addiction to sack,
Lunch, lunch is a unitary principle, as Balzac would tell you
And as any man of letters consulting his watch towards
noon
Would undoubtedly endorse. Lunch is the business of
capitals,
Whether in *L'Escargot Bienvenue, Gobbles*, or the cheap Italian
joint.
Impoverished or priggish in the provinces, where talent is
born,
The angry poets look towards London as to a sea of
restaurants,
Cursing the overpriced establishments of where they live
And the small scatter of the like-minded not on speaking
terms.
But even this pleasure has waned, and its sum of parts –
People shaking hands on the pavement, a couple entering
A taxi hailed in the London rain, the red tears on a bottle
And the absorbing conspiracies and asserted judgements
Of young men in the self-confident flush of their promise –
Its sum of parts no longer presents a street of epiphanies.
Too much now has been spoken, or published, or
unpublished.

[118]

Manias without charm, cynicism without wit, and integrity
Lying around so long it has begun to stink, can be seen and
   heard.
To come down south from the country in a freshly pressed
   suit
Is no longer the exercise in youthful if gauche dignity
It was once in days of innocent enthusiasm without routine.
And so I look forward to my tweed-clad solitude, alone
Beside a widening estuary, the lighthoused island
   appearing
Where waves of the sea turmoil against the river's waters
Baring their salty teeth and roaring. And here I can stand –
Forgive me my fantasies as, Lord, I surely forgive you
   yours –
In a pretence of being a John Buchan of the underdog,
With my waistcoated breast puffed against the wind. What
   do they long for?
Propping up bars with them I can pretend to be as they are
Though I no longer know what they are thinking, if ever I
   did,
And, raising this civil if not entirely sympathetic interest
In what they feel, I know it contributes little to them,
Adding, as it does, to a change in myself they might not
   notice,
Causing me this pain as I realize the way I must change
Is to be different from friends I love and whose company –
When the last carafe was ordered, an outrageous remark
   spoken,
Or someone announced his plan for an innovating stanza
Or a new development in his crowded sex-life – whose
   company
Was a landmark in my paltry accumulation of knowledge.
Perhaps, after all, this not altogether satisfactory
Independence of mind and identity before larger notions
Is a better mess to be in, with a pocketful of bread and cheese,

[119]

My hipflask and the *Poésie* of Philippe Jaccottet,
Listening to the sea compose its urbane wilderness,
Although it is a cause for fear to notice that only my
    footprints
Litter this deserted beach with signs of human approach,
Each squelch of leather on mud complaining, *But where are
    you going?*

Tannahill

Robert Tannahill, 1774–1810

'I would I were a weaver, I could sing all manner of songs.'
Shakespeare

Aye, Bobbie Tannahill, I'll brew
Unhappy truths of verse and you
In Scots lines of the turn and screw.
 Aye, Tannahill,
This reckoning is overdue,
 Lamentable.

We sang your songs in Paisley's school,
Ink-fingered Dux and classroom fool,
Each little lord of ridicule;
 Aye, Tannahill,
All learned your sweet and bountiful
 Melodic drill.

By singing you, I understood
That poetry's lax brotherhood
Lived in my town; and it was good –
 Aye, Tannahill –
To learn that verse did not exclude
 A local skill.

Blackboyds and yeltrins in the year
Seventeen hundred and seventy-four
Were ripe and brilliant, born to dare
 'The sin of rhyme'
That Burns committed in his pure
 Intimate crime.

In seventeen hundred and eighty-six
They set you learn a weaver's tricks
While Burns discovered Muses vex
    As well as grace,
Young Burns, whose Scots proprietrix
    Spat in his face.

Douce dandies of the posh salons
Took that man in, as if on loan,
Then having raised, they laid him down,
    Their ploughman poet.
They made Society's decision,
    And let him know it.

Burns, Tannahill and Fergusson,
These jorum-jirgers, they could hone
A merry R, lick till they shone
    Gently stroked Ls,
And then die young, or in Darien,
    Ink's asphodels.

Young dead like Leyden, Smith and Gray,
Unread, forgotten, sternly weigh
Against the doors of elegy
    And find them shut.
Timor mortis conturbat me –
    Not to forget.

An antiquarian of old airs,
You played your flute at Renfrew's fairs;
You sang of amorous despairs
    And country courting.
Aye, Tannahill, hurt love confers
    A sweeter singing.

[122]

Composing verses at your bench,
Lines woven inch by linen inch
To follow each iambic hunch
    Into its art,
You sang, like a beginning finch,
    Your common heart.

A wabster's craft would teach a man
To live with art as an artisan.
As you could weave, teach me to scan
    And turn a rhyme,
Fraternally, like Caliban
    His low sublime.

When Paisley's bodies sought to learn
At the Star Inn and the Sun Tavern,
You, Tannahill, taught them discern
    False verse from true.
They 'kenned y'r faither', and would turn
    Their wits on you.

Once set in print, that was enough;
Your melodies had had their puff,
Their papery chance. With each rebuff
    Your inkwells dried;
You, Tannahill, in local chaff,
    Were vilified.

My Tannahill, the delicate
Delight of poetry is to wait
And, suffering the alphabet,
    Allow songs come
The way a prodigal in debt
    Walks slowly home.

You could not wait, yet overheard
A fame that rarely is conferred –
Anonymously choristered,
    A song you wrote;
A farm-girl, singing as she sheared,
    Your song, her throat.

And still they are singing, by Gryfe,
By Cart, with gentle disbelief
In the lilt of words against life;
    And your words breathe
In the pianos, with a little laugh,
    Keeping their faith.

Gone, gone down, with a song, gone down,
My Tannahill. The tavern town
Said one book was your last and frowned.
    The River Cart
Ran deep and waste where you would drown,
    Your counterpart.

You clutched the papers of your tongue:
Gone, gone down, gone down with a song.
Pity the mad, darkened with wrong.
    Home Lycidas,
You died in the dish-cloth Cart, among
    The ugliness.

And in the morning schoolboys came
To fish for papers, speak your name
And take their landed catches home,
    Dried on the gorse;
Aye, Tannahill, boys caught your poems,
    Lost, watery verse.

[124]

By broom, by briar, by Craigie Wood,
Through Cart-side's river neighbourhood,
Your papers rotting on the mud,
   My Tannahill!
But the shelfie and the hawthorn bud
   You could not kill.

Green Breeks

J. G. Lockhart, *Memoirs of Sir Walter Scott*,
Macmillan, 1900. Vol. 1, pages 81–5.

Crosscauseway, Bristo Street, and Potterrow,
In Edinburgh, seventeen eighty-three –
    Boys there were poor, their social class was 'low';
    Their futures lay in work or livery.
Sir Walter Scott says they 'inhabited'
These streets they lived on; but, in George's Square,
    'The author's father' – so Sir Walter said –
    Did not 'inhabit' but 'resided' there.
Young Walter and his chums were organized
Into a 'company' or 'regiment'.
    A 'lady of distinction', who despised
    The ragged street-boys from the tenements,
Gave Scott 'a handsome set of colours', which
Made Walter grateful to that Highland bitch
Who'd later 'clear' her kinsmen from her land,
That Duchess-Countess named for Sutherland.

From Potterrow, Crosscauseway, Bristo Street,
The poor boys came to 'bicker' on the Square –
A military game, if indiscreet –
To thrash the sons of those 'residing' there.
Offspring of State, Law, Ministry and Bank,
With flag aloft, defended their regime
Against those 'chiefly of the lower rank',
Boy-battles at a simplified extreme.
Though vanquished from the subtly written book
That's history, the street-boys often won –
Scott says they did. Sir Walter undertook
Average lies in how he wrote it down –
Mendacious annals – that no one should forget
When beggars win, they're in the horsemen's debt;
And only Scott has chronicled their war –
A beaten boy becomes the conqueror.

One of his enemies, says Scott, was both
Ajax and Achilles of the Crosscauseway –
'The very picture of a youthful Goth' –
The first to fight and last to run away.
Blue-eyed, with long fair hair, tall, finely made,
That boy-barbarian awed him. Scott could tell
He and his class-mates mustered to degrade
This brave, presumptuous, vulgar general.
They called him Green Breeks, this boy whom Scott
    preserved
As a memento of his opposite
That, cheating him of what he led and served,
A novelist could have his way with it.
Scott draws the colour of his hero's eyes,
His shape, his height, but not the boy, who dies
Within the pickle of Scott's quickened prose,
Half-loved by Scott, half-feared, born to oppose.

In one fight, Green Breeks laid his hands upon
Sutherland's 'patrician standard'. Before
       He'd time to win it, he was faced with one
       Too zealous for 'the honour of the Corps'
Who had a hanger or *couteau de chasse*.
For honour, then, that boy cut Green Breeks down.
       To save a flag, the honour of his class,
       He struck him on the head and cut him down.
Imagined horsemen of the old regime
Transformed young Green Breeks to a Dying Gaul –
       A pictured history, the bronze of dream,
       A classic gesture in an urban brawl.
Scott's friend disgraced his 'regiment' and showed
Expedient dragoonship was its code.
Where was nobility? But Scott, you found
Your life's obsession on that cobbled ground.

Scott turned our country round upon its name
And time. Its history obeyed his whip
       When Scott sent out his characters to claim
       Their pedigrees in Green Breeks' leadership.
I do not understand, Scott, what you meant
By your displaced verse-prose 'nobility'
       Unless the tatters of your 'regiment'
       Were patched on Green Breeks, that, for chivalry,
Your heroes might go forth and look the part –
Part man, part prince, part soldier and part God –
       Ridiculous and lacking in support
       As, when they fall, mere modern men applaud.
But Scott, you failed; for where your Green Breeks lives
Is that dark tenement of fugitives
Who, fled from time, have no need to endure
The quicklime of your ordered literature.

Green Breeks did not inform. He kept his pride.
He nursed his lovely grudge and sword-cracked skull
    And took both pain and bribery in his stride.
    They offered cash, 'smart money', to annul
Shame and dishonoured laws. He would not sell
His wound: let them remember it. Scott says
    That childish purse was small – part comical,
    Part serious: the whole antithesis.
They would not meet him face to face, but stood
On dignity and used a go-between,
    Like states, transacting with the multitude,
    Who can negotiate, then intervene
With laws, with cavalry and troops, with style,
With system, representatives and guile,
Who, pompously, can compromise to win,
Pitch coins against a ragged ostentation.

Peasant baroque, like this, its nuts screwed tight
In praise of rabbles and those *sans culottes*,
    Won't change a thing. It whets an appetite,
    Unfankling truths inwoven like a knot.
It gestures like a ghost towards a ghost,
And, bringing Green Breeks back, or trying to,
    It reckons with desire, the human cost
    In losing what was old, and fierce, and true.
What did he do? Where did he live, and die?
That life can be imagined. I let him *be*.
    He is my light, conspirator and spy.
    He is perpetual. He is my country.
He is my people's minds, when they perceive
A native truth persisting in the weave
Of shabby happenings. When they turn their cheeks
The other way, he turns them back, my Green Breeks.

[129]

Green Breeks accepted what he asked them give –
A pound of snuff for 'some old woman – aunt,
    Grandmother, or the like', with whom he lived.
    Kindness, like courtesy, must ever haunt
Love-raddled reminiscence, Walter Scott.
You cannot hide behind mock-epic prose
    Your love of 'haves', amusement at 'have-nots'.
    Between your lines, it's easy to suppose
Deeper affections generate each word
Recalling Green Breeks in your years of fame.
    You drank toasts to his name in Abbotsford,
    Proposed to Green Breeks, not his father's name.
Be not amused, Scott. Go, and give him thanks
He let you patronize his 'lower ranks'.
Go, talk to him, and tell him who you are,
Face to face, at last, Scott; and kiss his scar.

Ode to a Paperclip

When I speak to you, paperclip, urging you
To get a move on and metamorphose,
You sit there mating with the light that shines
Out of your minerals, a brighter glint
Where, rounding at a loop, you meet the sun.
Paperclip, I like you, I need you.
Please, turn into something wonderful.
  I remember restless clerks, in boring places,
Unbend you to caress their ears, tickling
Their lobes, or, slowly, linking you until
They forged one of their office necklaces –
A daisy-chain, from flowers of the desk;
Or straighten you, to dab at inky fluff
Mossed round a comma or an asterisk.
  You have more uses than your name pretends.
Intimately fingered all late afternoon,
Frustrations weave you into metal knots,
Boredom's insignia in the typing-pools.
A secretary, composed but fidgeting,
Was once chastised with airborne paperclips,
But no one noticed what was being thrown.
  A box of you, when brought up from the store,
Then opened, looked at, looks like dying sprats,
All life in its pathetic multiples.
But these are not your proper transformations.
Who knows what purpose you'll be made to serve
When a suspender is in deep crisis, or
The manager's braces tear his buttons off?
  It's you they think of first, because they know
Your versatility can be delivered
On bodice straps or snapped elastics.
It's your neutrality that gets me down –

Disarming. Why do you do it? You work
On dictats to the underlings of death
As readily as you fasten up the drafts
   A democrat compiles on human rights.
Good and/or bad, important/unimportant –
Little survivor, you go where you're sent,
On memoranda from the Chiefs of Staff
To Ministers of State, down to the note
A man finds clipped inside his wage packet,
Saying, *Sorry, you've been made redundant.*
   You also get lost and nobody cares.
It's part of your status to turn up in
A handful of change, or to appear from
Her handbag when she's powdering her nose.
You've no prestige at all, a tiny one
Among the commonplace, the vacuumed millions,
Diminished things, the meek disposables.
   Hand-made gold-plated paperclips do not,
I am sure of it, get made, let alone
Presented at executive goodbyes,
Although I've seen a breasty typist wear you
As earrings and, on her, you looked like treasure.
More than familiars, more than desk-top trinkets,
You're precious, though we may not choose to say so.
   Give them gold watches or cut-glass decanters,
It's you they're likely to remember as
The days go by, watched from their patios,
As, too, they think of Miss-What-Was-Her-Name –
Evasive, leggy and impertinent –
The one who worked gymnastic, sculptural
Designs in wire, her secretarial art.
   Ubiquitous, docile and mass-produced,
Existing in relationship to work
And tedium expressed thereof, you are
As functional as roads or pen and ink.

A box of you, when shaken on the ear,
Can make Brazilian noises, a rhythmic sea,
Plural as salt, as leaves, as citizens.
   Ghost-bullets, triple-loops, no matter what
Inquiring minds might call your outline capsules,
You change your shapes and will go anywhere,
Do anything for a piece of the action.
Immoralist! Turncoat! Mercenary!
You don't need her, or him – Love me; love me,
And go where I go, gentle talisman.

The Deserter
Homage to Robert Desnos

'Somewhere in the world, at the foot of an embankment,
A deserter parleys with sentries who don't understand his
*   language.'*

At the world's end, just before everything stops,
There may not be a war going on, but it is where
Broken lines of contested frontiers converge,
Drawn long ago by the hands of shrewd statesmen
In the years when they bagged the knees and elbows of
    their suits
In the grandest of all the world's capital cities.

It is at this place they keep the railway carriages
Of armistice and treaties, those waggons which brought
The revolutionary and his bales of pamphlets.
Many cattle trucks rot on a spread of sidings
With their memories of last kisses, of goodbyes,
A child's hand in yours, his eyes under the skip of his cap.

This is the last mortuary, the bottom inch of six feet,
Home to pallid garrisons sustained on cigarettes
And fantasies of strangers, wrapped in greatcoats
The way the inflexible uphold their ideologies.
Their freezing breath fastens them as if by chains
To a heaven above the arc-lamps, above innocent airliners.

Snow has begun to fall on the guilty secrets of Europe.
Here, where the lines meet, and emplacements rise up
Out of mined earth in their laurels of wire, a man,
Unarmed, talks with another five who hold their guns
On him. This conversation is composed of cloth,
Of buttons, stars, and boots. Of wood. Of steel. Of wire.

'A spectre in a well-tailored shroud
Smoked a cigar at the window of his apartment.'

We have seen him, this upright father
Who has the stately manners of a priest,
Who, when he lets it slip, behaves like a tycoon
In armaments, believing that they died
In Buchenwald for capitalism, for him.

We have dined with this stranger, talked at meat
With him after the funerals of our fathers.
Our wives are fond of him. They have been known to
Abscond to some Swiss chalet with him where
He keeps the instruments of pleasure.

How confidently the ash balances on
The tip of his cigar, a grey drool;
And with what contempt for his possessions
He lets it fall . . . We have seen him in cafés,
Served, as if he has only to wave his hand.

We are asked to die for him, and we die.
In the unlikeliest places, we have died,
Places we never dreamt of sending postcards from.
There, in his red resorts, men vanish in
Factories that grind through men and native parishes.

Never to die, not even in the grand style
Tended by nieces married to Counts and Princes,
But to live always, at the concept of wealth,
In galleries and in the regularity of verse,
In metronomes pledged to custom,

And in the regulation of wages and bread,
Never to die. O with how much passion
We can condemn this man many have died for.
He claims even to love nature.
He praises its brutality as he hunts.

In his mouth is the taste of Europe,
Its rank saliva. When I see this ghost,
I am afraid of him, who, from his window,
Spits on the lives of so many people,
On my mother, my father, my wife, my friends, myself.

'A widow in her wedding-gown gets into the wrong train.'

>   So much is average, so much
>   That anyone can buy or touch,
>   Things you can watch, or put to sleep,
>   That walk, or run on wheels, or creep.
>
>   Other things are just mistaken,
>   Marriages, or wrong trains taken.
>   A widow in her wedding-gown
>   Alights somewhere, in the wrong town.
>
>   O Lady, run, it's over now,
>   Whatever grief that marked your brow
>   With something like a brilliant star
>   To tell this city who you are.
>
>   I shall possess your soul, bereaved
>   Of everything for which it lived.
>   I am a specialist of tears.
>   I weep the world's, let me weep yours.

I listen to the song you sing
About two lives, two wedding-rings.
I listen as you fold your dress
To the mute curves of your nakedness.

Ratatouille

I

Consider, please, this dish of ratatouille.
Neither will it invade Afghanistan
Or boycott the Olympic Games in a huff.
It likes the paintings of Raoul Dufy.
It feeds the playboy and the working-man.
Of wine and sun it cannot get enough.
It has no enemies, no, not even
Salade niçoise or phoney recipes,
Not Leonid Brezhnev, no, not Ronald Reagan.
It is the fruits of earth, this ratatouille,
And it has many friends, including me.
Come, lovers of ratatouille, and unite!

II

It is a sort of dream, which coincides
With the pacific relaxations called
Preferred Reality. Men who forget
Lovingly chopped-up cloves of *ail*, who scorn
The job of slicing two good peppers thinly,
Then two large onions and six aubergines –
Those long, impassioned and imperial purples –
Which, with six courgettes, you sift with salt
And cover with a plate for one round hour;
Or men who do not care to know about
The eight ripe *pommes d'amour* their wives have need of,
Preparing ratatouille, who give no thought to
The cup of olive oil that's heated in
Their heaviest pan, or onions, fried with garlic
For five observant minutes, before they add
Aubergines, courgettes, peppers, tomatoes;
Or men who give no thought to what their wives

Are thinking as they stand beside their stoves
When seasoning is sprinkled on, before
A *bouquet garni* is dropped in – these men
Invade Afghanistan, boycott the Games,
Call off their fixtures and prepare for war.

III

Cook for one hour, and then serve hot or cold.
Eat it, for preference, under the sun,
But, if you are Northern, you may eat
Your ratatouille imagining Provence.
Believe me, it goes well with everything,
As love does, as peace does, as summers do
Or any other season, as a lifetime does.
Acquire, then, for yourselves, ingredients;
Prepare this stew of love, and ask for more.
Quick, before it is too late. *Bon appétit!*

Loch Music

I listen as recorded Bach
Restates the rhythms of a loch.
Through blends of dusk and dragonflies
A music settles on my eyes
Until I hear the living moors,
Sunk stones and shadowed conifers,
And what I hear is what I see,
A summer night's divinity.
And I am not administered
Tonight, but feel my life transferred
Beyond the realm of where I am
Into a personal extreme,
As on my wrist, my eager pulse
Counts out the blood of someone else.
Mist-moving trees proclaim a sense
Of sight without intelligence;
The intellects of water teach
A truth that's physical and rich.
I nourish nothing with the stars,
With minerals, as I disperse,
A scattering of quavered wash
As light against the wind as ash.

from
Elegies

In Memoriam
Lesley Balfour Wallace Dunn
1944–1981

Second Opinion

We went to Leeds for a second opinion.
After her name was called,
I waited among the apparently well
And those with bandaged eyes and dark spectacles.

A heavy mother shuffled with bad feet
And a stick, a pad over one eye,
Leaving her children warned in their seats.
The minutes went by like a winter.

They called me in. What moment worse
Than that young doctor trying to explain?
"It's large and growing." "What is?" "Malignancy."
"Why *there*? She's an artist!"

He shrugged and said, "Nobody knows."
He warned me it might spread. "Spread?"
My body ached to suffer like her twin
And touch the cure with lips and healing sesames.

No image, no straw to support me – nothing
To hear or see. No leaves rustling in sunlight.
Only the mind sliding against events
And the antiseptic whiff of destiny.

Professional anxiety –
His hand on my shoulder
Showing me to the door, a scent of soap,
Medical fingers, and his wedding ring.

Thirteen Steps and the Thirteenth of March

She sat up on her pillows, receiving guests.
I brought them tea or sherry like a butler,
Up and down the thirteen steps from my pantry.
I was running out of vases.

More than one visitor came down, and said,
"Her room's so cheerful. She isn't afraid."
Even the cyclamen and lilies were listening,
Their trusty tributes holding off the real.

Doorbells, shopping, laundry, post and callers,
And twenty-six steps up the stairs
From door to bed, two times thirteen's
Unlucky numeral in my high house.

And visitors, three, four, five times a day;
My wept exhaustions over plates and cups
Drained my self-pity in these days of grief
Before the grief. Flowers, and no vases left.

Tea, sherry, biscuits, cake, and whisky for the weak . . .
She fought death with an understated mischief –
"I suppose I'll have to make an effort" –
Turning down painkillers for lucidity.

Some sat downstairs with a hankie
Nursing a little cry before going up to her.
They came back with their fears of dying amended.
"Her room's so cheerful. She isn't afraid."

Each day was duty round the clock.
Our kissing conversations kept me going,
Those times together with the phone switched off,
Remembering our lives by candlelight.

John and Stuart brought their pictures round,
A travelling exhibition. Dying,
She thumbed down some, nodded at others,
An artist and curator to the last,

Honesty at all costs. She drew up lists,
Bequests, gave things away. It tore my heart out.
Her friends assisted at this tidying
In a conspiracy of women.

At night, I lay beside her in the unique hours.
There were mysteries in candle-shadows,
Birds, aeroplanes, the rabbits of our fingers,
The lovely, erotic flame of the candlelight.

Sad? Yes. But it was beautiful also.
There was a stillness in the world. Time was out
Walking his dog by the low walls and privet.
There was anonymity in words and music.

She wanted me to wear her wedding ring.
It wouldn't fit even my little finger.
It jammed on the knuckle. I knew why.
Her fingers dwindled and her rings slipped off.

After the funeral, I had them to tea and sherry
At the Newland Park. They said it was thoughtful.
I thought it was ironic – one last time –
A mad reprisal for their loyalty.

Arrangements

"Is this the door?" This must be it. No, no.
We come across crowds and confetti, weddings
With well-wishers, relatives, whimsical bridesmaids.
Some have happened. Others are waiting their turn.
One is taking place before the Registrar.
A young groom is unsteady in his new shoes.
His bride is nervous on the edge of the future.
I walk through them with the father of my dead wife.
I redefine the meaning of "strangers".
Death, too, must have looked in on our wedding.
The building stinks of municipal function.
"Go through with it. You have to. It's the law."
So I say to a clerk, "I have come about a death."
"In there," she says. "You came in by the wrong door."

A woman with teenaged children sits at a table.
She hands to the clerk the paper her doctor gave her.
"Does that mean 'heart attack'?" she asks.
How little she knows, this widow. Or any of us.
From one look she can tell I have not come
With my uncle, on the business of my aunt.
A flake of confetti falls from her fur shoulder.
There is a bond between us, a terrible bond
In the comfortless words, "waste", "untimely", "tragic",
Already gossiped in the obit. conversations.
Good wishes grieve together in the space between us.
It is as if we shall be friends for ever
On the promenades of mourning and insurance,
In whatever sanatoria there are for the spirit,
Sharing the same birthday, the same predestinations.
Fictitious clinics stand by to welcome us,
Prefab'd and windswept on the edge of town

Or bijou in the antiseptic Alps,
In my case the distilled clinic of drink,
The clinic of "sympathy" and dinners.

We enter a small office. "What relation?" he asks.
So I tell him. Now come the details he asks for.
A tidy man, with small, hideaway handwriting,
He writes things down. He does not ask,
"Was she good?" Everyone receives this Certificate.
You do not need even to deserve it.
I want to ask why he doesn't look like a saint,
When, across his desk, through his tabulations,
His bureaucracy, his morbid particulars,
The local dead walk into genealogy.
He is no cipher of history, this one,
This recording angel in a green pullover
Administering names and dates and causes.
He has seen all the words that end in -oma.
"You give this to your undertaker."

When we leave, this time it is by the right door,
A small door, taboo and second-rate.
It is raining. Anonymous brollies go by
In the ubiquitous urban drizzle.
Wedding parties roll up with white ribbons.
Small pools are gathering in the loving bouquets.
They must not see me. I bear a tell-tale scar.
They must not know what I am, or why I am here.
I feel myself digested in statistics of love.

Hundreds of times I must have passed this undertaker's
Sub-gothic premises with leaded windows,
By bus, on foot, by car, paying no attention.
We went past it on our first day in Hull.
Not once did I see someone leave or enter,
And here I am, closing the door behind me,
Turning the corner on a wet day in March.

France

A dozen sparrows scuttled on the frost.
We watched them play. We stood at the window,
And, if you saw us, then you saw a ghost
In duplicate. I tied her nightgown's bow.
She watched and recognized the passers-by.
Had they looked up, they'd know that she was ill –
"Please, do not draw the curtains when I die" –
From all the flowers on the windowsill.

"It's such a shame," she said. "Too ill, too quick."
"I would have liked us to have gone away."
We closed our eyes together, dreaming France,
Its meadows, rivers, woods and *jouissance*.
I counted summers, our love's arithmetic.
"Some other day, my love. Some other day."

The Kaleidoscope

To climb these stairs again, bearing a tray,
Might be to find you pillowed with your books,
Your inventories listing gowns and frocks
As if preparing for a holiday.
Or, turning from the landing, I might find
My presence watched through your kaleidoscope,
A symmetry of husbands, each redesigned
In lovely forms of foresight, prayer and hope.
I climb these stairs a dozen times a day
And, by that open door, wait, looking in
At where you died. My hands become a tray
Offering me, my flesh, my soul, my skin.
Grief wrongs us so. I stand, and wait, and cry
For the absurd forgiveness, not knowing why.

Birch Room

Rotund and acrobatic tits explored
Bud-studded branches on our tallest birch tree,
A picture that came straight from her adored,
Delightfully composed chinoiserie.

She was four weeks dead before that first
Green haunting of the leaves to come, thickening
The senses with old hopes, an uncoerced
Surrender to the story of the Spring.

In summer, after dinner, we used to sit
Together in our second floor's green comfort,
Allowing nature and her modern inwit
Create a furnished dusk, a room like art.

"If only I could see our trees," she'd say,
Bed-bound up on our third floor's wintry height.
"Change round our things, if you should choose to
                                        stay."
I've left them as they were, in the leaf-light.

Writing with Light

A *dadaiste* tomboy, she'd fill a jar
Then hold it to the sun. The art of day
Leapt on the shapely glass, the unfamiliar
Blues, changes, clouds, a watery display
That calmed and caught clear heavens in a jar.

And damn the hand-washing. She'd run the tap,
Filling her jar, then hold it to the sun.
That contemplated water formed a trap
To catch the sky with. Experimental fun –
A jar, a sky, the flowing cold, a tap.

Mischievous girl – but she would dress so well.
I'd see from out our bamboo bed of love
Her fine unfolded clothes heaped where they fell,
And shoes, a hat, a stray unpartnered glove,
Discarded earrings, for she dressed so well.

And as for art, then she could write with light,
A rational, surreal photography
Reconjuring a world in black and white –
A pond in a box, a tabletop of sea.
I see her in the dark, writing with light.

Best friend and love, my true contemporary,
She taught me how to live, then how to die,
And I curate her dreams and gallery.
Writing with light, the heart within my eye
Shines on my grief, my true contemporary.

Tursac

Her pleasure whispered through a much-kissed smile.
"Oh, rock me firmly at a gentle pace!"
My love had lusty eagerness and style.
Propriety she had, preferring grace
Because she saw more virtue in its wit,
Convinced right conduct should have glamour in it
Or look good to an educated eye,
And never more than in those weeks of France
Perfected into rural elegance,
Those nights in my erotic memory.
I call that little house our *Thébaïde*
(The literary French!), and see her smile,
Then hear her in her best sardonic style:
"Write out of me, not out of what you read."

Empty Wardrobes

I sat in a dress shop, trying to look
As dapper as a young ambassador
Or someone who'd impressed me in a book,
A literary rake or movie star.

Clothes are a way of exercising love.
False? A little. And did she like it? Yes.
Days, days, romantic as Rachmaninov,
A ploy of style, and now not comfortless.

She walked out from the changing-room in brown,
A pretty smock with its embroidered fruit;
Dress after dress, a lady-like red gown
In which she flounced, a smart career-girl's suit.

The dress she chose was green. She found it in
Our clothes-filled cabin trunk. The pot-pourri,
In muslin bags, was full of where and when.
I turn that scent like a memorial key.

But there's that day in Paris, that I regret,
When I said No, franc-less and husbandly.
She browsed through hangers in the Lafayette,
And that comes back tonight, to trouble me.

Now there is grief the couturier, and grief
The needlewoman mourning with her hands,
And grief the scattered finery of life,
The clothes she gave as keepsakes to her friends.

At the Edge of a Birchwood

Beneath my feet, bones of a little bird
Snap in a twig-flutter. A hundred wings
Adore its memory, and it is heard
In the archival choirs now where it sings.

Ewes nurse their lamb-flock on an upland field.
Late gambols in the last kick of the sun
As I scoop dirt on a hand's weight, briefly held,
A cradled cup of feathered, egg-shelled bone,

Turning the earth on it; and underground
Go song and what I feel, go common things
Into the cairn of a shoe-patted mound,
Goes half my life, go eyes, instinct and wings.

The moon rubs through the blue pallor of high east
And childlessness has no number in the May
Shadowed with birchlight on the county's crest.
This year her death-date fell on Mother's Day.

At Cruggleton Castle

The trees stepped back into a giant mist.
A razorbill was a little lookout
In the binoculars, alone on its ledge.
Green, blue and yellow, the Bay dealt
Its sunken mirrors under the little boats
In a shuffle of sea-glass.
A Gallovidian palette, colourist,
Gathered its greeny pinks and evening blues
From the light in the middle of our lives.
Good minutes make good days. Good days make years.
A breeze dried on my lips; the Solway slapped
Against the cliffs of Cruggleton.
Wind in her hair, the wind composing her;
The wind entangled in her summer dress
Flew from her over the land, womanly.
Doves in a kirkyard slumbered on the stones.
That dusk was pure, pictorial, painterly,
An innocence, a loss, a life away.

The Clear Day

Sunlight gathers in the leaves, dripping
Invisible syrups. Long afternoons
Have been reduced to this significant
Table, melodious ice cubes shaken in
A blue tumbler, lazily tipped vermouth
And a hand measuring it, a propped elbow,
A languid eye, while a reflection on
A leaf turns into everything called summer.
The heat haze ripples through the far away
Gardens of strangers, acquaintances, of those
I can put a face to. With my eyes shut,
Squeezing the soft salts of their sweat, I see
Beyond my body, nerves, cells, brain, and leisure.
Blue coastal persons walk out of the haze.
They have outflown the wind, outswum the sea.
I think, and feel, and do, but do not know
All that I am, all that I have been, once,
Or what I could be could I think of it.
These blue pedestrians bruise the edge of me
To a benign remorse, with my lessons.
With my eyes shut, I walk through a wet maze
Following a thread of sounds – birdsong in
Several cadences, children, a dog-bark,
The traffic roaring against silence as
A struck match drowns it out, simple tunes of
An amateur pianist, a vulgar shout,
A bottle tapped against a thirsty glass,
The burst of its pouring, and the slip
When the chilled glass wets a wet lower lip.
I could not guess at what the pictures are
In the eyes of a friend turned round to watch
Shrub shadows dapple a few yards of lawn

As his smoke clings to his thoughtful posture.
Tonight, I shall look out at the dark trees,
Writing this in the muddle of lost tenses
At an o'clock of flowers turned colourless.
Then, as always, the soul plays over mind
With radiantly painful speculations.
I shall sieve through our twenty years, until
I almost reach the sob in the intellect,
The truth that waits for me with its loud grief,
Sensible, commonplace, beyond understanding.

A Summer Night

Dusk softens round the leaf and cools the West.
Rhythmical fragrances, wind, grass and leaves,
Fly in and out on scented cadences.
I go into the bedroom of the world,
Discovering the long night of my life.
This telephone is electronic lies,
Ringing with calls, with farewells of the dead
Paid for on credit. Nocturnal postmen ring
My doorbell; I refuse to let them in.
My birch trees have their own two lives to lead
Without our love, although we named them us.
They play inside the aromatic wind
That is their house for ever. Outside time,
On the sensation of a memory
I walk through the dark house, remembering.
I meet the seasons on the stairs, breathing
Their pulchritudes, their four degrees of heat,
Four shades of day, shade on shade, shade on shade.
I have gone through a year, in at one end,
Out at the same way in. Same every year,
But that year was different. I counted days
As Francis counted sparrows, being kind to them.
They were not kind to me. My floating life
Borrows its fortitude from a cool silence
Composed of green, from two trees, from the tingle
That was the touch of us against the world.
It left its lived heat everywhere we'd been,
A small white cry, one last wild, stubborn rose.

Reading Pascal in the Lowlands

His aunt has gone astray in her concern
And the boy's mum leans across his wheelchair
To talk to him. She points to the river.
An aged angler and a boy they know
Cast lazily into the rippled sun.
They go there, into the dappled grass, shadows
Bickering and falling from the shaken leaves.

His father keeps apart from them, walking
On the beautiful grass that is bright green
In the sunlight of July at 7 p.m.
He sits on the bench beside me, saying
It is a lovely evening, and I rise
From my sorrows, agreeing with him.
His large hand picks tobacco from a tin;

His smile falls at my feet, on the baked earth
Shoes have shuffled over and ungrassed.
It is discourteous to ask about
Accidents, or of the sick, the unfortunate.
I do not need to, for he says "Leukaemia".
We look at the river, his son holding a rod,
The line going downstream in a cloud of flies.

I close my book, the *Pensées* of Pascal.
I am light with meditation, religiose
And mystic with a day of solitude.
I do not tell him of my own sorrows.
He is bored with misery and premonition.
He has seen the limits of time, asking "Why?"
Nature is silent on that question.

A swing squeaks in the distance. Runners jog
Round the perimeter. He is indiscreet.
His son is eight years old, with months to live.
His right hand trembles on his cigarette.
He sees my book, and then he looks at me,
Knowing me for a stranger. I have said
I am sorry. What more is there to say?

He is called over to the riverbank.
I go away, leaving the Park, walking through
The Golf Course, and then a wood, climbing,
And then bracken and gorse, sheep pasturage.
From a panoptic hill I look down on
A little town, its estuary, its bridge,
Its houses, churches, its undramatic streets.

Land Love

We stood here in the coupledom of us.
I showed her this – a pool with leaping trout,
Split-second saints drawn in a rippled nimbus.

We heard the night-boys in the fir trees shout.
Dusk was an insect-hovered dark water,
The calling of lost children, stars coming out.

With all the feelings of a widower
Who does not live there now, I dream my place.
I go by the soft paths, alone with her.

Dusk is a listening, a whispered grace
Voiced on a bank, a time that is all ears
For the snapped twig, the strange wind on your face.

She waits at the door of the hemisphere
In her harvest dress, in the remote
Local August that is everywhere and here.

What rustles in the leaves, if it is not
What I asked for, an opening of doors
To a half-heard religious anecdote?

Monogamous swans on the darkened mirrors
Picture the private grace of man and wife
In its white poise, its sleepy portraitures.

Night is its Dog Star, its eyelet of grief
A high, lit echo of the starry sheaves.
A puff of hedge-dust loosens in the leaves.
Such love that lingers on the fields of life!

[162]

Home Again

Autumnal aromatics, forgotten fruits
In the bowl of this late November night,
Chastise me as I put my suitcase down.
The bowl's crystal shines and feels like frost,
And these have been the worst days of its life.
Cadaver orchard, an orphanage of pips,
Four apples sink into a pulpy rust,
And *Eat me, eat me*, says a withered pear,
Pay for your negligence and disrespect.
A scent of Burgundy – a bunch of grapes
Drinking their mortuary juice, their wrinkled skins
Dwindled and elderly black emaciations.
My six weeks gone from home portray the days
On stopped clocks and a vegetable absence.
Throw out the green loaf and bacterial cheese,
Shrunk carrots and potatoes begging for earth.
It is very lonely on the green settee,
Under the lamp, with my breath visible.
The curtains dangle in a window-sway,
In window-cold. I touch their foliage,
Their textile, sympathetic park.
I have been there in dreams, walking among
Peach-groves, and dressed in raiment of the East
In vineyards overlaid with Martagon lilies,
Arabic gardens, the south of Summerland.
Warmth is beginning and the pipes shudder.
I taste my house. Each day of its hungry gnosis,
It led a life of its own, empty of me.
The moon's oasis, the moon sipped the fruit
And the dust settled and thickened, the cold
Entered books and furniture, china and cushions.
My open suitcase mocks me from the floor.

[163]

The room is an aghast mouth. Its kiss is cold.
I think of a piano with its lid locked
And a carved, ivory silence in it.
I look at a vase. It is too much to bear,
For it speaks of a deranged expiry,
An accusation of browned leafage.
I see the falling off of its petals
In a flashback of flowers, the white zig-zags,
A snowfall of botanic ecstasy.
A spirit shivers in the appled air,
And I know whose it is. A floral light
Bleaches my eye with angelophanous
Secrets. They are more than remembering,
Larger than sentiment. I call her name,
And it is very strange and wonderful.

The Stories

No longer are there far-flung outposts of Empire
   Where a heartsore widower could command a wall
Against the hairy raiders ignorant of commerce.
   Too much morality has interposed
Its wishy-washy journalism and hope. Who am I
   To weep for Salvador or Kampuchea
When I am made the acolyte of my own shadow?
   Grief has its own romance, its comedy,
Its preposterous and selfish gestures. Men and women,
   Who, one day, will feel as I do now, I
Empty my heart, my head, dreaming again of days
   Gone by in another life. I could sail North
To Spitzbergen, to the iced-over mountainous islands
   Outlined on charts of the glacial deltas,
Or south to the rainforests, or to the blank of sands
   Drifting like the heartlessness of time.
Where is the frontier I could serve with a paid sword
   Dutiful to an imperial ass who lavishes
His days on orthodox, abstruse theology
   And his exchequer on a paradise
To please the gluttony of his heretical consort?
   At my age, I could die splendidly on
A staircase, unarmed, banished, but soldierly, before
   The spears and sabres of the wicked host
That trumped my preparations and stole the city
   In the name of their Prophet. I could have died
On the trails of exploration, under the sun or the arrows.
   And what religion is left now, to serve
With local Caledonian sainthood, stern, but kind,
   Baptizing the baby Africans, and plodding
To a discovery of God and waterfalls?

Nor are there any longer those unvisited isles
Where a beachcomber might scrounge a boozy salvation.
To meditate in a tropical hovel –
Palm leaves, creeper, coconut shells, jettisoned
                              containers –
On wheretofores, buts, ifs and perhapses,
Over that anguished prose of what we think we deserve,
Or don't deserve, but live with, either way,
Would be a perfect if anti-social philosophizing,
Doubtless illogical, or arrogant,
Or windily puffed-up to heights of self-deception.
Interior ethics, like oncogenic catastrophes,
Happen anywhere, the melanomas of the sun
Or the occult surprises of contemplation.
Why grieve like this? I loathe my bitter, scorning wit,
This raffish sorrow artificed by stories.
I can see myself in a jungle-drunk's smeared linen suit
Under the fan in a lost trading post,
Most Maugham-ish in my matutinal repartee
At my breakfast of mango and whisky
As the steamer arrives, delicate with white nuns
And crates of Haig and quinine, the new clerk
Already mothered on the rack of a malarial fever.
There are a thousand plots in the narrative
In which grief is the hero. In these frequent stories
There is always somewhere to go to, outbacks,
Exiles, White Men's Graves where piratical gun-runners
Mix with evangelists, where wilderness
Brings out the worst of men as well as charity,
Where sacrifice embroiders every tale
And the devoted nun weeps in the shot-up pagoda
As a Chicagoan's lung-blood soaks her arms.
Breast-plated with Gustavus Adolphus and Dalgetty,
I could have lost myself in Baltic syntax.
Foot-slogging the Sahara with kepi, pack and gun,

[166]

I could have made the beautiful gesture,
The joke of spitting in Death's broad, fictitious grin.
It is no longer the world of the stories.
Opportunities for a ludicrous public service,
    For the lunacy of last-ditch duty
To Monarch, regiment or John Company,
    Are stoic options stored in Yesterday.
Why be discreet? A broken heart is what I have –
    A pin to burst the bubble of shy poetry,
Mnemosyne revealed as what, in life, she stands for.
    I shall observe the moods of the great sky,
The flight of herons, the coming into leaf of birches
    And the religious glow on ancient waves
Breaking against *Candida casa* of the cliffs.
    If you should see me, or one of my kind,
Looking out to the far ocean from a lonely headland,
    Or walking by the hedgerows, then turn away.
Walk on by, and leave us there to remember and dream
    Our speculative visions of the past
Narrated through the legendary, retrospective fictions,
    Tales of anachronism. Such days they were!
Not even that sweet light garnishing Sisyphean innocence
    Redeems me, dedicated to the one
Pure elegy, looking as if I like the way I am.
    I do not; for I would rather that I could die
In the act of giving, and prove the truth of us
    Particular, eternal, by doing so
Be moral at the moment of the good death, showing
    An intimate salvation beyond the wish
Merely to die, but to be, for once, commendable.

Anniversaries

Day by nomadic day
Our anniversaries go by,
Dates anchored in an inner sky,
To utmost ground, interior clay.
It was September blue
When I walked with you first, my love,
In Roukenglen and Kelvingrove,
Inchinnan's beech-wood avenue.
That day will still exist
Long after I have joined you where
Rings radiate the dusty air
And bangles bind each powdered wrist.
Here comes that day again.
What shall I do? Instruct me, dear,
Longanimous encourager,
Sweet Soul in the athletic rain
And wife now to the weather.

Glaswegian starlings fly
In their black cape, a fluttered noise,
Ornithological hurrahs
From spires in the November sky.
   The Candleriggs is husks
And cabbage leaves, a citric scent,
A vegetable sentiment,
Closed apple-depots in the dusk's
   Indigenous metaphor –
Arcadian orchards of the lost
On this Bohemian sea-coast
And exits, pursued by a bear.
   I passed our wedding day
Drunk on the salad street, a null
White-out of loss and alcohol;
Your ring, our anniversary,
   And starlings in my soul.

   A liquid light sips dew
From how it is as blossoms foam
With May's arboreal aplomb
Against a reminiscent blue.
   Day, number, memory,
Kissed hours when day's door hangs ajar
And light crawls on the calendar,
Each routine anniversary
   At night, and noon, and dawn,
Are times I meet you, when souls rinse
Together in their moist reunions.
Iambic, feathery Anon
   Opens anthologies,
Born and reborn, as days go by
In anniversaries of sky
When oceans cradle little seas
   That water in the eye.

My diaries are days,
Flesh days and real. The calendar
Recurs to tell us who we are,
Or were, to praise or to dispraise.
  Here is a day come round
Again. This window's a wet stone
I can't see through. Daylight and sun,
Reflectionless, a glassy ground,
  It slides on vitreous space.
I shiver in the memory
And sculpt my foolish poetry
From thwarted life and snapped increase.
  Cancer's no metaphor.
Bright rain-glass on the window's birch
This supernatural day of March,
Dwindled, come dusk, to one bright star,
  Cold and compassionate.

Hush

Shh. Sizzle of days, weeks, months, years . . .
How much of us has gone, rising and crying.
My skin seeps its pond of dew.

Air sips and licks as I walk out today
In the transparent jaw of the weather
When the first leaves are greening.

Behind me I can hear
A click of fantasy heels,
But there is no one there.

She is with me, as I call to see
A sick friend whose skin is drying
On the bones of her spirit.

I stand on the sad threshold with my flowers.
How old this is, and how the heart beats faster
As I wait at the bell like a mourning wooer,

As the dog barks, as I give my flowers
And a secret wind blows in from eternal woods,
As my flowers sigh, asking for water.

Leaving Dundee

A small blue window opens in the sky
As thunder rumbles somewhere over Fife.
Eight months of up-and-down – goodbye, goodbye –
Since I sat listening to the wild geese cry
Fanatic flightpaths up autumnal Tay,
Instinctive, mad for home – make way! make way!
Communal feathered scissors, cutting through
The grievous artifice that was my life,
I was alert again, and listening to
That wavering, invisible V-dart
Between two bridges. Now, in a moistened puff,
Flags hang on the château-stacked gables of
A 1980s expense account hotel,
A lost French fantasy, baronial.
From here, through trees, its Frenchness hurts my heart.
It slips into a library of times.
Like an eye on a watch, it looks at me.
And I am going home on Saturday
To my house, to sit at my desk of rhymes
Among familiar things of love, that love me.
Down there, over the green and the railway yards,
Across the broad, rain-misted, subtle Tay,
The road home trickles to a house, a door.
She spoke of what I might do "afterwards".
"Go, somewhere else." I went north to Dundee.
Tomorrow I won't live here any more,
Nor leave alone. *My love, say you'll come with me.*

from
Northlight

For Baba and Robbie

At Falkland Palace

For L.J.B.

Innermost dialect
Describes Fife's lyric hills,
Life, love and intellect
In lucid syllables,
        Domestic air.
Natural play of sun and wind
Collaborates with leaf and mind,
        The world a sentient
        Botanic instrument,
                Visible prayer.
Everything's birth begins
On the moment of the May's
Creaturely origins
– I'll live for these good days
        Love leads me to
In gardened places such as this
Of the flower and apple-promise,
        Lark-sung, finch-wonderful;
        Edenic circumstance, not fall,
                Walking with you.
Balladic moments pass,
Tongue-tied, parochial,
A narrative of grass
And stone's hierarchical
        Scottish Versailles.
These native liberties propose
Our lives, rose by unbudding rose,
        A song-crazed laverock
        Whose melodies unlock
                Audible sky.

Dynastic stonework flakes,
Weathers and fails, withdraws
From shapely time and shakes
A gargoyle's severed claws
          At visitors.
Here wrinkled time's abolished house
Perpetuates a posthumous
          Nation, monarchy's urn
          In which the Stewarts mourn
                    What once was theirs.
          In a country like this
          Our ghosts outnumber us:
          A ruined artifice
          Empty and sonorous,
                    Malevolent
In how its past force-feeds with filth
Anachronism's commonwealth
          And history bemoans
          What history postpones,
                    The true event.
          In the hollows of home
          I find life, love and ground
          And intimate welcome:
          With you, and these, I'm bound
                    To history.
Touching your hair, holding your hand,
Your beauty blends with time and land,
          And you are loveliness
          In your green, country dress,
                    So fair this day.

Love-making by Candlelight

Skin looked like this two hundred years ago
When candlelight lapped the erotic straw
In hilly farms where windowed candlefire
Burnished imperfect glass. Portending haws
Hung on the leafless bush, amazement's bud
Red on the acres of nocturnal snow
As uplands rose to tufted winterlight,
In their celestial altitude
The eighteenth-century stars.

This is how it must be, shape-shifting fire's
Impatient nudity and ours
On the big bed. A molten vividness
Dismantles gender and the way it moves
Identifies a married venery
Timeless in the bedroom of the species –
A Pictish smile, a medieval kiss,
A whispered pre-industrial draught
On our contemporary bed.

Played on by fire, those clustered cornice grapes
Outwit their plaster: cornucopia's vine,
Pompeian opulence, rumours
From far back, echoes of Florentine
Intrigue, Renaissance footsteps in the hall
Where gossips overhear indelible
Echoed courtships; and these Muscovian furs
Were linen until fire reshaped
Their transient destiny.

[177]

Hands dipped in light-and-shadow cast
Ledas and satyrs on the bedroom wall.
A candleflame's a silent chatterbox
And cinematic book: bestiary candle,
History candle, yellow metaphor,
Venereal fire. Open the curtains now
And add a star to what we do and say
Past midnight in our only country,
Our private anywhere.

Who else is looking at the Firth tonight
Drowsy with afterlove? Local Tristan,
Indigenous Iseult, and Dido sees
Aeneas in a navigation light.
Dog-collared Abelard walks Heloise
Among the gravestones, yews and cypresses.
An Orphic nightbird cries 'Eurydice'. . .
Love, touch my heart with who you are
And sleep, history, sleep.

S. Frediano's

S. Frediano is St Finnian
Who spelled the rivers with his wand of faith,
The Ayrshire Garnoch and the streams of Down.

He brought his water-miracles to Tuscany,
Turning the Serchio with a little rake,
Praying, perhaps, when it was done, in Gaelic.

Lucca was lonely but not foreign
Far from his college on the coast of Solway,
Candida Casa's Gallovidian stone.

He lies under the high altar
In a faint aroma of cypress,
His bones united by fine silver wires.

It is cool and dark in S. Frediano's church.
Parishioners pray in its visited sanctity,
Listlessly pious, old, *simpatico.*

Tourists listen in on telephones
To stories in the language of their choice.
There is that smell of medieval history.

I hear a bird high in a vitreous blur
Singing its song of the sacred windows,
Its coincidental literature.

S. Zita, mummified, is dressed
For blessed waltzing when the trumpets sound.
Her skin is fastened like a frozen dust,

Her fingerjoints a grey bamboo,
Her gown a lace spun by celestial spiders,
Bridal, bizarre, miraculous.

In her glass coffin, she exhibits
Centuries of death that mount and mount.
Light Italian lire clink in the coinboxes.

It is a human place – a tourist
Stooped in a pose of scholarly inspection;
A couple who light candles for their dead

And who have yet to read
S. Frediano learned his miracles
In places they came here to be away from.

The People Before

I've turned my back on Tuesday's half-past four
As 1985's obscured momentum
Falters towards the closing of an epoch.
Crepuscular, two tradesmen, walking home,
Know that they're woodcuts by a local master,
Firm local lines, modernity unstuck.

Migrating geese, in an up-ended V,
Caricature my watch's measurement,
Half-past the hour and continuity
In sepia, any time but this
Post-dated country etched in aquatint
Nearing the day of luck and all good wishes.

Streetlamps come on.
Frock-coated decades trespass on the tense.
Spent eras stain
Anachronistic stone –
Luminous echoes, gaslit reminiscence,
Distorted, thinned, Victorian.

A push can coax our gate
Into releasing an Edwardian squeak.
December's frozen rose
Nods to unseen applause.
A sparrow lifts its startled featherweight
And petals tumble in a cruel slapstick.

Preliminary moonlight on the Firth
Casts in-betweenness on the time and light –
Not now, not then, not day, not night,
But moonlight's childhood, waterworn;
And, in one moment, all death, all birth,
All dying and being reborn.

Beyond our neighbours' frosted washing-lines,
Their silvered slates and chimneypots,
Our borderland begins
As light withdraws to loss of Monifieth,
Subplots and counterplots
Narrated in the coastline's myth.

Make what you can of it, for no one knows
What story's told by winter-misted hills
Or how a river flows
Against the tide in white scribbles.
A patiently daemonic frost
Sharpens its needles on the eastern coast.

Processionals of lives go by
On delicate, crisp treads;
Blurred fragrances, gently percussive,
Stir among leaves.
Top-hatted heads of firms and kitchen-maids
Visit the instincts of the eye.

Swish, hush and microsound, the whispered *ahs*,
Converse with silence's midpoint
Over the Firth, and time is disobedient,
Mixing its years and generations.
It's 1940 on the weatherglass
And now and then in the events of nations.

Night swells with navigation's stars
Honed to a masterpiece of quiet.
Dismantled commerce hungers for its jute,
Esparto, timber, coal and mariners,
Prosperity and credit.
Lighthouses warn the swimmers on a lost trade route.

A candleflame, held by a child
Walking past, reddens a window, her face
A spectral captive in the window's glass,
Her neck a ruff of fiery nightgown lace.
Coniferous estates, the winterfield,
Submerge their farms in foliage and grass.

More geese rant westward, flock by chevroned flock.
The house of us now, love, of you and me.
I turn a blacksmithed key in its lock.
Feeling its freezing metal on their hands,
These other people turned this iron key.
The lunar honey fell on Buddon Sands.

February

Maternal in the glow of shaded light,
Your smile has proved the truth of love tonight,
Holding the hunger of our much-loved child
Who lately in his father's arms was held.

Daylight

The big white arms of dawn are cool
In their embrace, and merciful
First blue dispels the estuary's
Possessive, tenemented greys.
The gleam on Buddon Ness protects
Survival where sunlight reacts
With sand and private history,
With window-coloured dawn and sea.
Enormous world, this little place
Observes its vulnerable trace
On time, topography and globe,
Its rooftops polished in the scrub
Of climbing sunlight, while the gleam
On Buddon Ness persists, a dream
In sleepy eyes at windows where
Early risers pause and stare
At distances beyond their town,
And someone in a dressing-gown
Eavesdrops as mysteries discuss
Sung mornings to no human purpose.
Wordless symposia, in tongues
Informed beyond mere rights and wrongs;
Luminous discourse, shade by shade,
Its meanings light-and-water-made
Or turned by wind and by what happens
Into a foliated sense –
A mind could catch at them, and try
To understand that dot of sky
Balanced on Buddon's easternmost
Outreach of military coast

Transmitting random ironies
Out of the library of days.
I've seen a star poised on the tip
Of a still leaf, pure partnership
Here makes with there and everywhere
Between life, death and forever.
Last night in Tayport, leaf and star
– Still, very still – melted together
In life's delight and woke to this
Lucidity and genesis,
A worldlight in the watery grey,
Sinister, thrawn, the estuary
A colourless mirroring stone,
Offensive, querulous, sullen;
And then daylight on Buddon Ness,
Curative, clear and meaningless.

75°

I

Delayed by southern possessiveness,
The summer's agents turn up late
With their sorries, their more-or-less
Sincere apologies, lightweight
Attire, ubiquitous assistants
Performing aerial events,
Weavers of avian cradles where
A byre or gable tucks the air
Under its eaves. 'What kept you, friends?'
Bavarian asparagus,
Burgundian grapes and other godsends,
The usual Hispanic fuss,
Devonian nativities
Beginning in the apple trees.
The glass farms of the Netherlands
Commanded sun and tied our hands.
'At least, you've come. Our bad selves, dulled
By winter and frustrated spring,
Drained good from us, and poured a cold
Malevolence over everything.'

II

We tend our earthen restaurants,
Buying our portions of the south;
Strange languages visit our tongues,
Saying 'I love you', mouth to mouth.
Erotic gardens promise fruit
Nurtured from an ancestral root.
A smile, and the clematis flowers.
A few weeks more, and south is ours!
Yachts multiply; pods flex
Deserved and succulent harvests.
Lawn-mowers, shirt-sleeves, open necks . . .
Young girls ring daisies round their wrists.
Mrs Belle Gilsand's parrot squawks
For liberty beyond her clock's
North-facing mantelpiece – humdrum,
Tick-tocking tropic martyrdom.
Deep in coniferous woods, the dry
Needle blankets shift, claw and squall
Shaded by wing-beats, then a shy
Creaturely panic and paw-fall.

III

Eat fern seed, walk invisible.
Summer is fragrant this far north.
By night, on Inverdovat's hill,
Visit the gods of wood and Firth
By paths of inner wanderlust
Here on the summer's Pictish Coast
Where half-forgotten festivals
Quicken the half-remembering pulse.
Watch starlight struggle in an oak's
Irradiated rafters, hear
A minstrelsy from lunar hammocks
Sing love songs to the hemisphere.
Moonbathe, be moonstruck, watch a birch
Assume serenity and search
For its perfection, northern
On its grass sofa, turf and moon-fern
Delighted where a foot-snapped twig
Startles symphonic foliage
And mushrooms tremble on their log,
Stellar on an eternal ridge.

IV

The heart stays out all night. Each house
A variant of moonlit slates
And flightpaths of the flittermouse,
Sleeps in the dream it illustrates
Translating garden laureates
Into unlettered alphabets,
Holding antiquity and now
Within the same nocturnal vow –
Internal wonders in that pale
Hour after sunset when you hear
A visionary nightingale
Articulate your life's frontier.
An owl perched on a chimneypot
Too-woos its legendary thought
Across the estuary of dream
Along the light-buoy's punctual beam.
Stars in the trees, moon on a headstone,
Night's footprints on the riddled earth;
The wind's herbaceous undertone,
Moon-puddled water, mystic Firth . . .

V

Planthouses force Italian heat
On melon, pepper, peach and vine
And horticultural conceit
Perfects a Scottish aubergine.
Imagination manufactures
A vitreous continent, nature's
Geography turned inside out
On the botanic roundabout.
By fraudulent, glass-roofed lagoons
Gardeners ply the trowel and hoe
On Polynesian afternoons
Of the oriole and the papingo.
Waterfalls slacken, their cold threads
Dribble on shrunken riverbeds.
There's trouble at the reservoir:
At night it launders one pale star.
Dry pelts diminish on the road,
Each beast its dehydrated shroud;
A butterfly's life-episode
Withers in daylong adulthood.

VI

Postponed by seasonal delight
And midnight sun, the north returns,
A furred, Icelandic anchorite
Travelling south by landmarked cairns,
Islands, headlands, bearing his cold
Autumnal charms, spelling ridged gold
Into the shiver in the leaf,
Deciduous, wrinkled and skew-whiff.
Rumoured by clouds and sudden chills,
By falls of apple, plum and pear,
Arched, orphaned cats on window-sills
And by botanic disrepair –
Look to your blessings and your coat,
Gloves for your hands, a scarf for your throat.
Your gardens, yielding pod by pod,
Surrender to another god.
Go home; chop wood. North-easters strain
Over the sea. Farewell. This line –
Greybreaking, late September rain –
Falls heavy, cold, and argentine.

Here and There

'Everybody's got to be somewhere.'
Woody Allen

You say it's mad to love this east-coast weather –
I'll praise it, though, and claim its subtle light's
Perfect for places that abut on water
Where swans on tidal aviaries preen their whites.
You whisper in the south that even the rain
Wins my affection, and I won't deny it,
Watching it drench my intimate domain:
I love the rain and winds that magnify it.
The evening's paper-boy goes round the doors
At his hour of November when the day's
Closing in goose-cries and the sycamores
Darken to silhouettes by darker hedges –

I love that too. *'Provincial'*, you describe
Devotion's minutes as the seasons shift
On the planet: I suppose your diatribe
Last week was meant to undercut the uplift
Boundaries give me, witnessed from the brae
Recording weather-signs and what birds pass
Across the year. More like a world, I'd say,
Infinite, curious, sky, sea and grass
In natural minutiae that bind
Body to lifetimes that we all inhabit.
So spin your globe: Tayport is Trebizond
As easily as a regenerate

Country in which to reconstruct a self
From local water, timber, light and earth,
Drawing the line (this might please you) at golf

Or watersports on a sub-Arctic Firth.
It matters where you cast your only shadow,
And that's my answer to, *'Why did you choose*
Grey northland as your smalltown El Dorado?
You've literature and a career to lose . . .'
It isn't *always* grey. And what is grey?
A colour like the others, snubbed by smart
Depressives who can't stroll an estuary
Without its scope of sky bleaching their hearts.

'. . . You'll twist your art on the parochial lie.'
I love the barbed hush in the holly tree.
'An inner emigré, you'll versify,
Not write. You'll turn your back on history.'
Old friend, you're good for me, but what I want's
Not what your southern bigotry suspects.
Here on imagination's waterfronts
It's even simpler: fidelity directs
Love to its place, the eye to what it sees
And who we live with, and the *whys* and *whens*
That follow *ifs* and *buts*, as, on our knees,
We hope for spirit and intelligence.

Turbulence reaches here: the RAF
Loosens the earwax – so, not paradise
Unless you're awkward, Tory, daft or deaf
Or dealing in destruction's merchandise.
I hold my infant son at the window.
Look, there's the blue; I show him sky and the leaf
On the puddle. What does a baby know
Of the hazardous world? An acrid *if*
Diseases happiness, the damned *perhaps*
Perfected by the uniforms of State.

Our sunlit roofs look nothing on their maps
Other than pulverable stone and slate.

A ferry town, a place to cross from . . . Verse
Enjoys connections: fugitive Macduff
Escaped Macbeth by it. Lacking his purse,
He paid in bread – The Ferry of the Loaf . . .
'Ferries? Fairies! That's medieval farce!'
The wizard, Michael Scot, was born near here . . .
'I might have guessed you'd more like that, and worse . . .'
. . . Alchemist, polymath, astrologer
To the Holy Roman Empire; Tayport's son
Mastered all knowledge, too controversial
For Dante who invented his damnation
In the *Inferno*: 'Tayport Man in Hell,'

They'd say in the *Fife Herald* – 'Sorcerer
From Tayport Slandered by Tuscan Poet.'
*'Worse than parochial! Literature
Ought to be everywhere . . .'* Friend, I know that;
It's why I'm here. My accent feels at home
In the grocer's and in Tentsmuir Forest.
Without a Scottish voice, its monostome
Dictionary, I'm a contortionist –
Tongue, teeth and larynx swallowing an R's
Frog-croak and spittle, social agility,
Its range of fraudulence and repertoires
Disguising place and nationality.

*'What's this about Tayport's centenary?
I never thought you'd prime a parish pump.'*
Not me. Who's said I have? *'It's scenery
You're there for.'* No, it isn't. *'Mugwump!'*

[195]

You're wrong again, old friend. Your Englishness
Misleads you into Albionic pride,
Westminstered mockery and prejudice –
You're the provincial, an undignified
Anachronism. The Pax Britannica's
Dismissed, a second-rate Byzantium,
Self-plundered inner empire's Age of Brass.
No houseroom's left in the imperial slum.

And as for scenery, what's wrong with love's
Preferred country, the light, water and sky
Around a town, centennial removes
From time? – The universe within the eye,
Cosmogyny, not parish-governed stars
Cultured above the Tay, but seen from here
When late-night amateur philosophers
Puzzle the substance of their hemisphere.
Time, space and yours truly: all men deserve
Somewhere, if only that, fruition's place,
Quotidian but extra, on a curve
That's capable of upwards into grace,

Eccentric elegance, the personal life
Sharing its ordinariness of days
With speculative spirit which is midwife
To nation, intellect and poetry's
Occurrence. *'You're looking for a chance to wear
A three-piece suit in tweeds with heavy brogues,
Rehearsing presbyterian despair
On a shoreline, in Reithean monologues.'*
So what, if I talk to myself in the woods?
*'Perverse retreat into the safe and small
Suggests fake self-denial.'* These latitudes
Enlarge me, comfort me, and make me whole.

[196]

'No, you're evasive, knowing it might be wrong
To hedge ambition into quietude
That serves a lowered will with local song,
Beachcombing an iambic neighbourhood.'
It serves my loyalty. It serves increase.
I'll keep no secrets from you: it serves love;
It serves responsibility and caprice.
Damn all careers; I'd rather *be* than *have*.
'You mean, it serves you right?' I hope so, friend.
Pay me a visit and we'll drink to life
One evening when the light and water blend
On the conjectural points of coastal Fife.

Come by the backroads with a sense of time.
Come like Edward Thomas on a holiday
In search of passages of wild-flowered rhyme
No Scot or Irishman would dare betray.
Now, though, I'm going out to the black twigs,
Shy waterbuds reflecting as they drop
To the neighbourly, where the good ground swigs
Any libation from its earthen cup.
Scottishness, if you say so; but I see
Plurals and distances in voiceless wet
Enough to harbour all my history
Inside a house protected from regret.

December's Door

in memoriam Philip Larkin

I kept a church leaf, wishing it were blossom.
    Hull's undressed roadside sycamores
Waded through brittle drifts from Cottingham
    To Newland Park, the still striders.
That leaf still marks my place, but it was worn
    Before I put it there; now dust
Dirties the page, and sinews, strong as thorn,
    Impress the paper's softer crust,
Fragments hanging from them, leaves of a leaf
    Preserved into a second autumn.
Afterwards' keepsake, its botanic grief
    Crumbles in death's *ad infinitum*.

A rudimentary, unclouded sky:
    That day in Hull, your funeral,
I watched rubescent figments vitrify
    On library windows, unreal
Emblems of warehoused English literature
    On the Fifth Floor, and saw again –
When I was in my twenties, I worked there –
    Hull's hazily Utopian green
Purpled and pinkened in a luminous
    Record of seasons. Long straight roads
Reached out across nocturnal Holderness,
    The sea and the visitless woods.

A leaf-marked book aches on my windowsill.
    Straw gold and central green were there
A year ago, but book-locked winterkill
    Disfigured them in printed air.

In a closed shadow, opened now, a door
    Into December's estuary
Beneath a wigged moon, it honeys the floor
    To starry oak, reflected Tay.
Geese draw their audible, Siberian bow
    Over the moon and Buddon Ness,
And now I can't repay the debt I owe,
    A withered leaf, a dry distress.

Sorrow's vernacular, its minimum,
    A leaf brought in on someone's shoe
Gatecrashed the church in muffled Cottingham,
    Being's late gift, its secret value
A matter of downtrodden poetry,
    Diminutive, and brought to this
By luck of lyric and an unknown tree.
    A passer-by was bound to notice
Crisp leaves at work when everyone had gone,
    Some fricative on paving-stones
As others flecked a winter-wrinkled lawn,
    Remote, unswept oblivions.

Winkie

'We also serve'

GIVE ME GOOD PIGEONS!
You pose in your glass case
Putting a brave face on your taxidermed
Municipal afterlife.
Close by you, Winkie, is a photograph,
A bomber's aircrew snapped in the Second War.
You were their mascot and survival kit.
    Click-click went their tongues;
    And *Winkie-Winkie* they sang
Pressing titbits through the wooden bars
On leather and vibrating fingers.
Winkie-Winkie chirped the goggled men.

Over Norway, its fuselage and wings on fire,
The bomber droned down to the sea,
    Flames sizzling in sleet
    As frantic signals pinged
Against deaf radio ears in nowhere.

Cupped hands released you from a rubber boat.
    Miniature of instinct,
    Dedicated one, your stuffed breast swells
    With pride in your only nature!

GIVE ME GOOD PIGEONS!
Their *chuck-chuck-chuck's*
A thwarted cooing from the woods
Haunting city squares
Named for dimwits and dignitaries
With old bucolic neighbourhoods,
Fife, Gowrie and the Mearns.
Whether as spy-birds on a sneaky errand
Bearing a snip of microfilm for eyes
Devoted to secrecy, released by a hand
Clandestinely over a window-sill in Warsaw,
Or with the gentler mail of love, birth and death
Winged over the suburbs and snipers from
The besieged city – see the rifle, the Prussian eye
Point through the foliage round the gardened villas –
    You are liberty's bird,
    Unstreamlined and civilian,
    With the guts and stamina of a taxpayer
And behind you the solidarity of your species,
    The Universal Union of Pigeons.

    Your mission doesn't matter
    Nor what unvisa'd coasts
    You cross on your postal expeditions,
Nor the direction you take, or whatever
Nationality is claimed for the forests below
Or who pretends to own the air and seasons
And the pronunciation of rivers and mountains.
    The blame is not yours –
    Docile legionary,
    Warrior bearing words,
    Beloved of the Intelligence Services'
    Eccentric dogsbodies,
    Dovecote attendants

[201]

In the obscurest ministerial spires
With their bowls and jugs, their bags of maize
For kept cushats, *pigeons voyageurs*, homers,
Birds of the cloak-and-dagger cryptography.

An imprisoned lover turns on his stinking straw
And a dove at the window chortles.
A letter is read to the sound of cooing.

I do not like the big brave boasts of war.
    GIVE ME GOOD PIGEONS! –
A very large number of Great Commoners
Built like Nye Bevan or Gambetta.

    Winkie read his charts
On his table of instinct, and found the Tay's dent
        On the planet of places.
        A perfect rescue – saved by a bird
        Homing down to Carnoustie.

Bird of X-marks-the-spot
Bird of the ringed foot, married to the miles
Bird of human purpose but immune to guilt
Bearer of tidings and long-distance billet-doux
Reports of troop movements, the planned assassination
Scorner of moats, guard towers and jammed radio
Dove that to a hand in Babylon
Brought more news of the strange horsemen
And bird that to Chaucerian casements brought
Melodious greetings to the heartsick Lady
Bird of the allotments, bird of the long race
Hand-held bird, heartbeat in gentle hands
Olympic bird, love-bird, bird of the peace
Dove of the Annunciation, forerunner of Christ

Bird of the strange beam and the beautiful lily
Mendicant bird, begging around footwear
With your jabbing head, your hungry, urban strut

FLY, WINKIE, FLY!

A House in the Country

'O God! I could be bounded in a nut-shell, and count myself
a king of infinite space, were it not that I have bad dreams.'
                                                    Hamlet

Not Scotland. The colour of the stone
Remembers somewhere *sur Vézère*
Or Tuscany, the Serchio's watertone
Italianate among the cocklebur.

Unopened years burst loose, an iron gate
Inched on its hindered arc, its squeak
Increasing as my bodyweight
Crushes its rust through cry to scream and shriek.

A sore path, and illegible:
Its arrow-headed thorns nip legs and hands –
Red-beaded bracelets and a scratched standstill
Waist-deep in brambled reprimands.

The door's decayed and locked: flaked paint and rust,
Negative timbers on which wood-weeds cling,
One in flower. A doorpost
Crumbles on toe-touch, shuddering.

A kick would smash this door.
I look around and wonder where I am,
Hearing my blood percuss, the red drummer,
Then find a key cold on my sweating palm.

Webs lace the narrow hall. Floorboards protest
At the weight of my shadow, disgruntled
Cries that release an insect ghost,
Digested flies on a transparent scaffold.

A joist gives on my afterstep. Wood quits
Its fastenings. House-sounds reverberate
In a grey resonance as powdery minutes
Clamour for quiet and then hesitate

On their hazards, blinking in light
Shuttered until now, sneaking
Through keyholes, under doors, off-white
On plaster puddles, the whole house creaking.

A sitting room's dust-sheeted furniture
Dwells on its family thoughts in indoor silence,
The frequency on which its spiders hear
Their lives and predatory conversations

Passing down lifetimes, polyphonic with
Remembered chit-chat or a chair's
Collected memories. Piano breath
Withdraws into its contemplated quavers.

Books and a desk; a jacket's shape
Transforms a chair into a studious shrug,
An amputated, headless stoop
Mouthing a dusty monologue,

Pulling the darkness down
As seasons, politics and swallows pass
And natural and human transformation
Recur on dusty window-glass.

In swirls of air and daylight alien
To it, reluctantly, the room confronts
Sky, wind and summer's herbal rain,
Noise, light and celebrants.

A grey globe ponders on its plinth,
A sphere within a varnished O's embrace
Hugging the planetary labyrinth,
Its cuddled continents all out of place.

Webs fold and curdle in the sunlit wind's
Expulsion of the shadows, and a man
Appears from nowhere or the mind's
Liberty to be more than one.

I am nowhere, everywhere and past
In a house in a country I do not know
A stone clock on the mantel grinds to dust
Minutes that were lifetimes long ago

'No, not that door,'
He says. 'Look at your mirrored face.
You'll learn you've visited that room before
In other houses in another place.

'Reality's the ghost
Stalking your privacy and footsteps
With minstrelsies. Your innermost
Identity eavesdrops

'On what it does and where it goes with you
Among the flowers and clocks, perfidy, faith,
The groves of rooms that utter you
Beyond the physical and into death.'

And then he says again: 'No, not that door.'
Skeletal alphabets
Drop from their bookshelves to the rubbled floor,
Trash *videlicets*

Dismembered from their etymologies,
Words and the shards of an unspoken word,
Lost mouths and dumb debris
Emaciated and disordered.

Hereafter's solitary, rooted to
His captive afterlife disturbed by me,
He spins his globe, and dust-clouds clear to blue
Oceans, greens continents and history.

Imagined stranger, I am in your house
By ways of sleep and owls, and you know why
The door you guard's the door I have to choose
Before my cowardice becomes a lie.

Jig of the Week No. 21

Under optimum conditions – the room quiet
In fireglow, rain lashing on nocturnal glass –
I start an old American puzzle.
It smells like my Webster's dictionary;
It reminds me of the lesson in Latin
Translating Lincoln's *Gettysburg Address*
Into my Ciceronian of errors.
On junior versions of wet, wintry nights
Around Christmas, I tried to be patient,
A jigsaw on a white enamel tray
Encouraging pictorial wanderlust –
My father's ear close to the wireless set's
Hummed murmuring of Cold War '49,
My mother sewing, my brother fast asleep.
Posed by the artist in a daze of stunned
Courage, a wounded man waves in the paint,
A salutation from a grassy foreground.
Here is a piece of sky; this one's a hoof.
I give a man his legs, then rummage for
A clue of horse, a clump of grass. Slaughter's
Perfectionists, the North Virginian troops
March through the woods of Pennsylvania
Intent on orders and aesthetic war.
Omniscient history makes good puzzles:
This one is *Pickett's Charge at Gettysburg*.
Jigsaw research – whose side was Pickett on?
I look him up, then file a book away.
The man who painted this supported Blue;
My mind and fingers soldier with the Grey.
Three hundred fragments of American

Cardboard carnage! This old Bostonian box
Crossed the Atlantic sixty years ago;
Thousands went all over the United States
Shipped by the Universal Distribution Company.
A segment finishes the Stars and Stripes
Carried before blue-trousered infantry.
A dozen pieces, more or less the same,
Assemble shell bursts, foliage and sky,
Turquoise and pink, a summer's afternoon
On Cemetery Ridge, the Butcher's Bill
Extortionate in fact but not in paint –
Invoices brought at night, slipped under doors.
A painter oiled his military bias,
For a good price, and then his work became
A reproduction of a reproduction
Issued in multiples, mail-ordered
All over childhood to the merry puzzlers.
You can open old wounds like a box,
That slow knitting of pictures and glory
In Tennessee and Massachusetts.
I hold an inch of space, the missing piece,
The notional and beautiful republic
Expressing what was fought for and who died,
'The last full measure of devotion . . .'
– Put hats on heads, place heads on fallen men
And resurrect the dead, the broken wheels:
A finished puzzle ends up in a dream,
A subterranean, consecrated picnic,
A hand waving in the fraternal paint.

4/4

in memoriam John Brogan

There was that night at pleasant Kate's
When you beat out your boogie'd bars
Among the bow-tied advocates
Swaying like minor characters
Of the Enlightenment, their laws
Dismantled by your drag and pause.
Your left hand's rhythmic boom and walk
Shivered the porcelain and crushed
Twelve strokes of midnight on the clock.
Even the chatterboxes hushed.
Like a young Hoagy Carmichael –
Thinking, smoking, drinking, sociable –
You used to stare out through your fug
With that half-smile of early wisdom,
Part intellectual, part rogue,
Pro life and *anti* tedium.
Here's to your memory, Jack,
Leaning into a whispered joke
Or a conspiracy against
Conservatives and sundry shits
Whose pranks or phoniness incensed
Distrust of the patriciates.
And here's to yesterday's State Bar
And to the socialism of pleasure;
Here's to that half-cut afternoon
Jamming at Jimmy's in Rutherglen
Until my beat-up tenor sax
Spat springs and pads, giving it max,
When Lithuania's silver flute
Whistled its lyric absolute.

Bohemians with haircuts, glass
In hand, the decent working-class
Created us for politics
In which we talked but couldn't lead,
Read poetry, played jazz instead,
Our undeclared republic's
Ferocity discussed and shelved
As notional and unresolved.
Strange how we served the cause of books:
Knowledge, a pike to stand behind
At barricades of love and mind –
Read this, and contradict the crooks!
This toast's to our librarianship –
I catalogue each taste and sip.
A drink, too, for our generation's
Withered ideals, that dwindled sense,
Sold out, tormented innocence
And salaried impatience.
So here's to booze's brotherhood
Puking on Ballageich Hill.
It didn't do us any good,
But what the hell, Jack, what the hell.

In-flight Entertainment

Time lets its scientific minutes drop
On the Australian emptiness, a brown
Rugged geology where clocks are baked
In God's kiln, earthenware timepieces
Computing natural spans of insect life
Anticlockwise. Marginal nature gets by
Where there's no one to go for a walk with
And the first and last footprints slid under
Into deserted time and dry grottoes
Yesterday or millennia ago,
It makes no difference. That town beneath us,
Without buildings, fencing or municipality,
Might be the place called Nevermore, a dry
Republic ruled by solar plutocrats.
Some clown crossed it on camelback, others
Discovered the dotted line of their hot trek
Staggering over the unwritten map
Into a parched waterhole, imagining
Their own bones posed as they would leave them,
Deliberate, heroic litter,
Dissolving into horror, then into spirit.
So, better to sit up straight, back to a rock,
And hope for dignity in the annals,
A winged shadow casting its event of shade
To the cries of lost nomads and explorers.
        At thirty thousand feet, it's all go now
In our flying cinema. Earphones bring me
Time whiled away in in-flight entertainment.
I choose the channel called Heavenly Choirs
In the programme, but I'm in the wrong mood

For celestial flutes and the twanged God-harp
Concertos commissioned by the airline.
An Indonesian turbulence brings on
Spontaneous fidgeting with seat-belt buckles,
Ashtrays, and, in one case, a rosary.
It's as anxious as disaster's soundtrack.
My drink rumbas across its trembling tray.
Schooners on the Conradian sea and Dutch
East Indiamen race for the sheltered bays
Tiny under volcanoes, spice-bundles tied
In palm-roofed warehouses by windy wharfs.
Our big bird flutters its mineral feathers
Going down by invisible staircases
Through tropical rain, our slow descent driven
Straight to the shopkeepers of Singapore
And the days when I clerked for Stamford Raffles
In his turbanned garrison, mastering
Malay and opportunities of The Straits.
This airport doesn't feel like terra firma,
More like a space station, a half-way house
Between the stars and British history.
        Dark now, all the way to London, and sleep
Goes by me on its glass sails, not stopping
Throughout these pages of our *bon voyage*.
Over the Bay of Bengal, I walk down
Aromatic corridors, and India dozes
Beneath three hundred tons of rapid weight
And people crossing the world in three bounds.
I can see nothing but sacred darkness
On the underside of the wind, a glow
Where cloudy light describes a multitude
Dreaming in its city, its electric bowl.
I fall into a cultured quarter-sleep,
One eye half-open like a crocodile's.

[213]

Fictitious light squirms on the movie screen
But absentmindedness narrates another tale.
Reality's make-believe, and that's its point:
I've dreamt myself into mistaken times,
Not where I am, but all over the place.
The present's just as bad – the clock's going back,
But everyone's fixed to biological forwards.
Their destiny, like mine, is to grow old
As fate, or pilot error, has it, weather,
Metal fatigue, or ghostly horsemen from
The Mogul Empire, riding the stratosphere.
We're all travelling from the twenty-ninth
To the twenty-eighth, still living in
Yesterday, which takes us to Bahrain,
Where I have never been before. Pirates
On perilous star-dhows swing from the moon's
Islamic sickle, serious, cut-throat Sinbads.

      High over Babylon and Nineveh,
Ancient astronomers observe our lights;
Soothsayers with the troops of Alexander
Read our high thunder as a sacred omen.
I remember my classics teacher saying,
'Ah, yes, the Hittites . . . Who were the Hittites, boy?'
And there they are, the Hittites, one and all,
To say nothing of Midas, Mithridates,
Phrygia, Pontus and the satrapies
In Europe's Asian antithesis.
Where else should turn up next on my agenda
If not Byzantium outlined in neon
Advertisements, Marmora, Bosphorus?
Now that we're all awake, I hear a fool
Refer to down-below as Istanbul.
Where has he been for these past thousand years?

Miletus once was mighty, long ago.
I drag an adage over the Roman Empire,
Its winter vineyards, olive groves and highways,
Nocturnal autobahns, palatinates.
Night-lights in the European bedroom yield
To dawn and England in November.
Stiff knees and sleeplessness: I saw no God
In my internal flying-time throughout
These indoor hours at mighty altitude.
Those on the other wing can see the Thames,
Westminster foggy and Big Ben at seven.
Change terminals, change planes, process the bags,
This London never could be north enough
For me and who I love and travel with
And who has slept through half of geography.

An Address to Adolphe Sax in Heaven

For Ted Tarling

That your great gift to human ears
Offended purist connoisseurs
Might not be weird, but that's the word
They thought described the sound they heard.
Though Berlioz defended it
Most maestros reprehended it,
While Richard Wagner's saxophobics
Call for a mouthful of aerobics –
Rassenkreuzungsklangwerkzeuge.
Unrhymable! It's on its own,
Your 'instrument of hybrid tone'.
Bizet in his *L'Arlésienne* –
A sound like lyric Caliban –
Raised eyebrows as he lowered the tone
With solos for a saxophone.
Parisian social experts feared
The sound of sex was what they heard,
Melodic monsters, Minotaurs,
Breaking down their bedroom doors.
Its complicated *quidditas*
Prognosticated future jazz.
Not what you had in mind, *cher Sax*:
Concertos, not yackety-yaks,
Were more your forte. You would love
The alto one by Glazunov,
Ibert's, or Pierre Max Dubois's
Alto-harmonious noise.

Bordellos and the regiments
Took greatly to your instruments.

Your lacquered cosmopolitans
Marched under hot, colonial suns,
And, in a room behind the bar
In Senegal or Côte d'Ivoire,
Melodies no conservatoire
Would ever countenance were played –
A Guadeloupan serenade
Or tune to set the heart astir
In an outpost of Madagascar.
Saharan saxophones! Annam
Transfigured by their 'priestly calm'!

    Think of the clarinets of France
With instrumental reverence! –
Hyacinthe Klosé and Leblanc,
Their breath, the fingerprints of song!
What better mouth as embouchure
Than one that says the word *amour*
Or when the clarinet's played low
Describes its sound as *chalumeau*?
Its 'simple system,' you, Sax, built –
So-called because it's difficult –
Found favour, but the laws of patent
Failed to discourage disputant
Competitors and plagiarists,
Invention's parasitic pests.
Not, though, your seven-belled trombone
That looked like the first telephone
Exchange, your *saxotromba's* freak
Ingenious *saxomblatarique*.
That elephantine hearing-aid
Ruptured and deafened those who played,
Or tried to, its enormous tones'
Almighty bass convulsions.

[217]

Critical slander and derision
Postponed, but couldn't halt, your mission.
Low audiences applauded it
And your alumni in the pit
Stood up and wiped wine-sweaty brows
Taking their own, and their master's, bows.
You hoped for an orchestral glory;
Destiny wrote another story –
Hack-blowers in the Music Hall
And quick-march guardsmen in the Mall:
Ignored for a symphonic part
You put an *oompah* into art.
Ballroom, night-club and bawdy-house
Were futures for your posthumous
Discovery, the sound of feet
Dancing and tapping, indiscreet
Lyricism in the glowing smoke,
Venereal riffs and blue heartache
In Harlem or in *Barrowland*
Where half the orchestra were canned.
So, Sax, profanity's the fate
Your instruments negotiate
Through New Orleans to Buddy Tate
While saxophonic venery's
Libidinous communiqués
Disclose that St Cecilia's just
A woman when it comes to lust.
From Buffs and Garde Républicaine
To Charlie Parker and Coltrane!
Trambauer, Hawkins, Chu and Bechet,
Lester, Sims and Cohn, and Wardell Gray,
Hodges, Webster, Rollins, Getz,
Lucky, Lockjaw, Dexter, Konitz
Brought oompah'd art to that fine pitch

Where music's an erotic itch
A fingernail's too blunt to scratch.
But Arnold Bennett thought his ear
Affronted by the tunes of beer.

Now look at you! From Aberdeen
To hamlets in the Argentine,
In Reykjavik and Birmingham,
Djakarta and Dar es Salaam,
High-stepping bands with majorettes
Play saxophones like martinets.
Your beggar with its inbuilt bowl's
Played in the cause of rock 'n' roll's
Electric millionaires, subfusc
Wee buggers with an urge to busk.

A genius who invents a noise
Adds to the store of sonic toys
That *Homo ludens* in his wisdom
Accepts into his playful system.
Adolphe, once close to suicide,
Cher maître, take your place beside
Celebrity whose household name
Is dictionaried in its fame –
Derrick, the hangman, Heinz's beans,
Kellogg's cornflakes, Levi's jeans,
Ford of the cars and Louis Braille,
Freud, Epicurus, Chippendale,
Marx and the verse Petrarch devised,
Martini, and the pasteurized,
Newtonian Law, the arch of Goth,
Mackintosh's sea-proofed cloth,
And Wellington, he of the boot,
Good, optimistic King Canute,

[219]

Fabian's tactics, Mills' bomb,
The Midas touch, Brummell's aplomb,
Platonic love, Macadam's roads,
Several diseases, Pindar's odes,
Darwinianism, Cardigan,
And J. M. Barrie's Peter Pan.
From saxophone quartets by Strauss
On days off from the Opera House,
Or works by Milhaud and Ravel
Or Villa-Lobos in Brazil,
To Lester leaping in possessed
By his brass-belled iconoclast,
The sound we hear is yours, Adolphe,
Posterity, its howling wolf,
Time salivating on a reed
And fingering at breakneck speed.

The Country Kitchen

Madame Moulinier used to bring
Two rabbits a week, and two hens,
Still warm, but throttled. The kitchen's
Cutlery lacked a decent knife
But I did the best I could, wishing
There was an animal-opener
The equal in convenience
To what you'd use on a tin of beans.
Blood seeped from the blunt incisions.
Peeling each portion of their skins
The sounds were slight, but bad, and such
I had to shut my eyes and whistle.
It felt like pulling plasters off your leg –
The pain and noise of skin and hair.
The heads were worst of all –
The ears, the eyes, the little mouths.
Blood leaked from the drainpipe.
The house was bleeding.
As for the hens, I plucked feathers
Among the trees, beyond the house.
It took most of an afternoon.
It looked like an Indian massacre
When I'd finished – shattered head-dresses.
We cooked them in the big pot, *sauvage* –
Shallots, a muslin bag of herbs
Gathered from the neglected gardens.
Some of these herbs were weeds and grasses.
The dug garlic was green, but good.
So was the garnish of young chives.
On evening walks, I used to watch

The rabbits stare back from their hutch,
Wondering which bunny was next;
And the hens pecking white dirt – *dot, dot,*
And then the scare of a footstep.
I asked a peasant to sharpen my knife
On the stone he used for his scythe.
It made it easier, and it didn't –
My hand inside a hen's dead warmth,
Or slitting open the rabbits,
My wife saying, 'Keep the kidneys!' –
Amateur kitchen pathology.
So I said, 'I'm sick of rabbit;'
And, 'Another hen and I'll cluck!'
That village is announced by a fine sculpture.
A stone woman holds a stone child.
The woman's name is 'Abondance'.
I saw abundance all right:
In her stone bowls were stone vegetables,
Chiselled salads, a petrified artichoke.
I looked with envy at the walnut trees
Flourishing in botanical liberty.
The fishmonger's van was maritime,
Cold, dripping with melting ice,
An edible museum of the sea.
For nights on end I dreamt of close quarters
Boxed behind the nailed mesh,
Creeping backwards into furred heat,
Packed eyes and lettuce breath,
When ringed fingers dropped in
On a carnivorous visit.

About the Author

Douglas Dunn was born in Scotland in 1942 and grew up there in the village of Inchinnan. He worked in libraries for several years before attending the University of Hull, from which he graduated in 1969. In 1971 he resigned from the library of the university to become a free-lance writer. He has been writer-in-residence at the universities of Hull, Dundee, New England (New South Wales, Australia), Duncan of Jordanstone College of Art, Dundee, and Dundee Central Library. Faber and Faber published his eight books of verse, the most recent being *Elegies* (1985), *Selected Poems* (1986), and *Northlight* (1988). Five of his books, including the most recent, were Choices of the Poetry Book Society (London), and he has received the Somerset Maugham Award, the Geoffrey Faber Memorial Prize, the Hawthornden Prize, the Whitbread Prize for Poetry, and several Scottish Arts Council Publication awards. *Elegies* was chosen as the Whitbread Book of the Year for 1985. Dunn has also published a collection of short stories, *Secret Villages* (Faber & Faber, and Dodd, Mead, 1985) and occasionally contributes fiction to *The New Yorker* and other publications. He has written plays for BBC radio and television. Since 1985 he has been lead book reviewer for the *Glasgow Herald* newspaper. He is currently completing *The Faber Book of Twentieth Century Scottish Poetry, The Oxford Book of Love Poetry,* and *The Collins Scottish Anthology.* Dunn is an honorary professor of the University of Dundee, and honorary fellow of Humberside College, a fellow of the Royal Society of Literature, and an honorary doctor of laws of the University of Dundee. He lives in Fife, Scotland.